MANAGERIAL ACCOUNTING

Applications and Extensions Using Lotus 1-2-3

Second Edition

MANAGERIAL ACCOUNTING

Applications and Extensions Using Lotus 1-2-3

Second Edition

Kathryn M. Verreault, Ph.D.
University of Lowell

Daniel A. Verreault, Ph.D.
University of Lowell

NOTE: This workbook uses problems from Dominiak and Louderback's Managerial Accounting, Fifth Edition, and Wolk, Gerber, and Porter's Management Accounting: Planning and Control (both, PWS-KENT Publishing Company), and is designed to accompany either of these textbooks. However, this workbook can also be used with any other standard, introductory managerial accounting textbook.

The data diskette required to work the problems in this workbook is not included. Instructors of classes using this workbook will provide information about distribution of the diskette.

PWS-KENT Publishing Company
Boston, Massachusetts

PWS-KENT Publishing Company is a division of Wadsworth, Inc.

Printed in the United States of America

1 2 3 4 5 6 7 8 9 -- 92 91 90 89 88

CROSS-REFERENCE OF PROBLEMS TO DOMINIAK & LOUDERBACK TEXT

AND WOLK, GERBER AND PORTER TEXT

PROBLEM	TOPIC	TEXT	PROBLEM
1	Contribution Margin, Taxes	D&L,4th	2-13
2	VCP Analysis - Product Mix	D&L,5th	4-21
3	Product Line Reporting	D&L,5th	4-29
4	Product Line Income Statements	D&L,5th	4-32
5	Joint Products	D&L,5th	5-16
6	Product Pricing - Off-Peak Hours	D&L,5th	5-24
7	Special Order	W,G&P	E12-1
8	Multiple Materials - Manufacturing Firm	D&L,5th	6-23
9	Budgeting For a Hospital	D&L,5th	6-31
10	Flexible and Static Budget	D&L,5th	6-33
11	Return Ratios and Leverage	W,G&P	E19-7
12	Production and Cash Disbursements Budgets	D&L,5th	7-9

TABLE OF CONTENTS

INTRODUCTION

This introduction will help you to get started with model-building using an electronic spreadsheet. We hope to give you 'the basics' which allow you to manipulate data and relationships, save and print files, and design logical spreadsheet formats. Please read this material carefully before starting your first project.

Application of Spreadsheets to Coursework

One very good reason to use spreadsheets in connection with your coursework is that knowledge of spreadsheets has practical value as discussed above. This is not the only reason, however. There are two important educational advantages for use of spreadsheets in accounting curriculums.

First, the use of spreadsheets encourages you to examine several sets of data for any given model. The student may then observe the effects of various ranges of data on the results of the model. You can then write about your choices based upon several sets of output. Slogging through several iterations of a problem by hand is neither practical nor much fun.

Second, in building a model, you are explicity forced to think about relationships involved in a certain area such as budgeting. The specific form of spreadsheet design we recommend requires that data (the numbers) and logic (the relationships) be stored in separate areas of the spreadsheet.

Level of Student Preparation

Until curriculums insist upon a more standardized approach to preparation of students in the use of microcomputer skills, there will continue to be a wide variety of backgrounds brought to the use of this tool. Some of you will know very little about spreadsheets, some will know a good deal. If you know very little, there is undoubtedly some difficult (but worthwhile) "start-up" time involved. You may select wrong commands, and have your whole spreadsheet disappear; you may become "trapped" and no matter what you do, the computer will only "beep" at you. Remain calm and ask for assistance. Chances are your error is minor.

We strongly feel that any start-up costs are well worth it in light of the advantages of spreadsheet knowledge discussed above. Find out from a knowledgable person, or by consulting the Lotus documentation, what you did wrong, document the solution, and don't repeat the mistake.

Finally, to get an introduction to the whole of Lotus 1-2-3, you may find it useful to use the interactive Lotus tutorial which is supplied with the program. Your lab probably has it available. The tutorial exposes you to all facets of the program, and may ease the transition to working with actual templates.

USER INSTRUCTIONS FOR LOTUS® 1-2-3®

The following instructions are provided to assist you in the successful use of this practice set. These instructions will provide you with the basics of Lotus 1-2-3, the prominent electronic spreadsheet used in the business world.

Our intent is not to turn you into electronic spreadsheet wizards, but rather to give you an exposure to some basic cost accounting applications utilizing the powers of the electronic spreadsheet. Your mission, should you choose to accept it, will bring you from the simple number-input stage to the development of logical spreadsheets. We credit you with the desire to understand the logic involved in the solutions as opposed to passive contentment with the blackbox approach. Good luck.

(Read all directions before beginning solutions.)

1. The Electronic Spreadsheet

The electronic spreadsheet is an organized grid of rows and columns. Any intersection of a row and a column results in a particular identifiable cell. The columns are denoted by letters and the rows by numbers. Therefore, C14 indicates the intersection of column C and row 14.

The power of the electronic spreadsheet rests with the ability to express relationships among cells and to change all related cells with predefined commands. The user can construct complex tables, schedules, etc., which are made of related cells. The user, in effect, constructs general relationships which solve particular problems-perhaps a budget. The more creative the user, the more complex the template (precon-structed relationships). The relationships may then be used many times by simply changing the data. "What if" analysis is encouraged. Lotus will compute, and you must think as a model builder and interpreter of results.

The Keyboard

The Lotus keyboard is illustrated on the next page. Several special keys will be particularly useful to you. First the pointer-movement keys (the arrow keys) allow you to move around the spreadsheet. Additionally, pressing the "Home" key returns you immediately to the upper-left corner (or beginning) of the spreadsheet. The "ESC" (escape) key also serves a special purpose. It allows you to back up through a series of commands or any keystroke. Finally the function keys serve a special purpose. Several, in particular are very useful to the Lotus operator. These will be discussed in the following section of this supplement.

The Keyboard

The keyboard includes four major parts (figure 2).

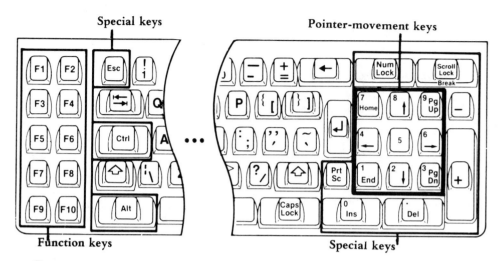

The Display Screen

The display screen of Lotus follows:

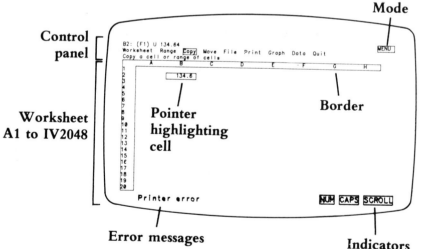

Source: Lotus Manual page 21

The Pointer highlighting cell indicates in which cell Lotus is currently accepting information. The "Mode" Lotus is in is indicated in the upper right corner of the screen. Examples of possible Lotus modes include: Label, Value and Menu. The "Indicators" on the lower right reveal if any special keys, such as [Caps Lock] have been pushed.

2

The Window

Given that the total Lotus worksheet has 256 columns and 2048 rows, only a small area or "window" can appear on the screen at any one time. An example of one of the many possible windows follows:

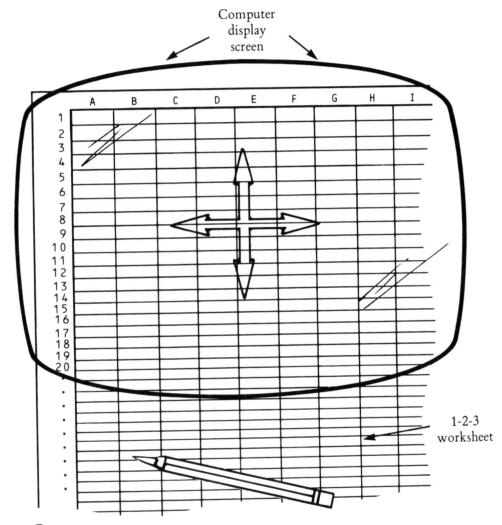

Source: Lotus Manual page 22

The Control Panel

The control panel serves to give the Lotus user information on 1.) the cell address currently used 2.) the characters of your entries as you type or edit and 3.) quick summaries of commands.

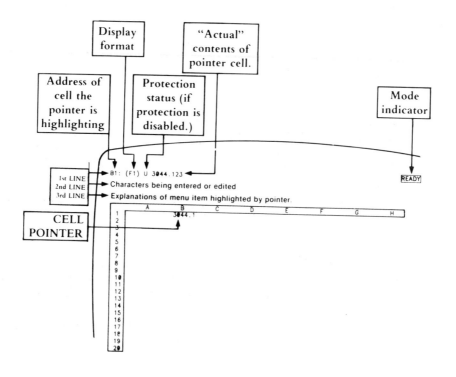

Source: Lotus Manual page 26

The Function Keys

The ten function keys located on the left of the key board perform specialized tasks in 1-2-3 as follows:

F1: [Help]	Display Help screen
F2: [Edit]	Switch to/from Edit Mode for current entry
F3: [Name]	In Point Mode, display menu of range names
F4: [Abs]	In Point Mode, make cell addresses "absolute"
F5: [GoTo]	Move cell pointer to a particular cell
F6: [Window]	Move cell pointer to other side of split screen
F7: [Query]	Repeat most recently specified Data Query operation
F8: [Table]	Repeat most recently specified Data Table operation
F9: [Calc]	Recalculate worksheet
F10: [Graph]	Draw the most recently specified graph

Source: Lotus Manual page 334.

F1,F2, and F5 are the three keys which you may find most helpful in completing these assignments. Consult the Lotus manual (or the help screens) to investigate the other function keys.

F1: (Help) displays information and instructions concerning the aspect of 1-2-3 which you are attempting. Some of the screens are better than others, but it is a good way to explore. If you want a hard copy of the particular help screen just press the "shift" and "Prtscr" keys simultaneously. This will "dump" the screen image to the printer. This is a good way to build a set of notes for your use.

F2: (Edit) the use of this key will be discussed in a later section. The switch works as a toggle; press it once and it is on, press it again and it is off. Lotus will sometimes put you in the Edit Mode when it doesn't like what you're telling it to do in the Ready Mode.

F5: (Go To) provides instant transportation around the worksheet. Simply enter the address after pressing the "F5" key, and Lotus will reposition the cursor at the selected cell.

Two Types of Lotus Menus

There are two types of Lotus Menus. They consist of 1. the line menu and 2. the stacked menu. The following paragraphs explain their significance.

The line menu consists of a number of menu options currently available to the user. They are displayed on the top of the spreadsheet in a horizontal line. The screen only typically displays part of the options available. To view the other options in the line menu simply press the right arrow key.

Stacked menus consist of the subcategories of options available within any line menu option. These are displayed when the particular line option is high-lighted. For instance, if you high-light 'File", you will notice you have further choices as to what to do with your file. You could 'Save', 'Delete', 'Merge', etc.

Pressing "Enter" while in Menu Mode in a multiple-line menu moves you a step further down the stacked menus. If you kept pressing "Enter" sooner or later you will be at the lowest level of a menu and Lotus will execute that command. If you discover that you are in the process of selecting a command you don't want and as long as 1-2-3 has not executed the command, you may recover pressing the "Esc" key. This key brings you higher up in the menu structure and ultimately back into the "Ready Mode".

2. Booting Lotus 1-2-3 and Selecting a Problem

Load the Lotus 1-2-3 System disk or System Back-Up disk
into drive I and close door.

Load the Problem disk into drive II and close door.

a.) If the machine is turned off, turn it on and the
machine will "boot" Lotus 1-2-3.

Press Return each time the red light in the disk drive
goes out until a blank spreadsheet appears.

b.) If the machine is on, press the Ctrl, Alt, and Del
keys simultaneously to "boot" Lotus 1-2-3.

Press Return each time the red light in the disk drive
goes out until a blank spreadsheet appears.

c.) If an A> appears on the screen, type 123 and continue
to press Return each time the red light in the disk
drive goes out until a blank spreadsheet appears.

Now you are ready to call up a template (preconstructed
problem) on the screen.

The next screen will tell you to press any key to
continue. Do it.

You are then provided with a blank template. To call up
an existing template:

(1) Press / - and you will have the Lotus 1-2-3 menu.

(2) Press the pointer key --> until "File" is highlighted,
and press Return, or else type F for File.

(3) You now have a new menu. The first choice in the menu
is "Retrieve". As you want to Retrieve a file and the
choice is highlighted, press Return.

(4) The next prompt is:

"Enter name of file to retrieve."

Again this can be done by typing in the name or scrolling
through the choices listed below, using the pointer key -->.
Once the appropriate file has been entered or highlighted using
the scrolling process, press Return, and that template will be
brought up on the screen.

You are now ready to solve the problem you retrieved.

You have brought up a copy of the template from the disk to

the active memory of the computer. The original template is
still on the disk.

3. Getting Around on the Worksheet

    To move the cursor (the high-lighted area which indicates
the cell at which Lotus is accepting information), use the
arrow keys.

To move right, left, up, and down:

    -->to move right   ↑ to move up
    <--to move left   ↓ to move down

    (If you hear a sound like a muffled beep, that means you
    have hit the boundary of the spreadsheet. Go the other
    way.)

4. Solving These Problems

Type A Problem

    It is important to solve and study Problem 1 or 2 (the Type
A problems). Wherever a cell has (NA) (indicating information
Not Available), you need to enter a value. (Note--solve the
problem in a logical manner, and you'll notice that some of the
(NA) values will be solved for you by the spreadsheet as you
fill in other information.) A copy of the template is attached
to the problem. If you have doubts about your ability to
choose a logical procedure to solve the problems, simply refer
to the template copy and solve the (NA)'s highlighted by a "#"
(i.e.# NA). The other (NA)'s will be solved by the computer.

    a)   Entering values: a few hints

        (1) Do not enter commas.
        (2) When entering a percentage, enter the decimal and
        three spaces (.333).
        (3) If a value should be zero, enter 0.
        (4) If you make a mistake--go back and fix it. The
        ESC key backs you up.
        (5) After entering any values (they appear on the
        upper left corner as you enter them), press an arrow
        key in the direction you next desire or Return. (This
        finalizes each entry to the computer, enters the value
        or label in the cell, and moves you to the next
        position.)

    b)   Editing Mistakes discovered after accepting your entry
        by pressing "Enter"

        Errors are sometimes discovered after you have
        accepted your initial entry. In this case, you may

proceed in one of two ways. Depending on the way in
which the error was discovered, i.e. by you or by
Lotus, and your own preferences.
1 If Lotus discovers your error:
   Lotus switches to the 'Edit Mode' from the 'Ready
   Mode'. The mode indicator is at the upper right
   of the display screen. In Edit Mode, you must fix
   the mistake as Lotus will not let you leave the
   cell until you do!

   To edit an entry:

   1. To edit a completed entry, move the cell
       pointer to the cell that contains the
       entry you want to revise. To edit an entry
       you are currently typing, start with step 2.

   2. Press EDIT. The mode indicator in the right
       corner of the screen changes to EDIT.

       Use the pointer-movement keys to move the
       cursor around in the entry.

   3. Insert or delete characters at the cursor
       location. (Delete with the Back Arrow key
       on the right top row of keys.)

   4. Press RETURN to complete the entry. The cursor
       can be anywhere in the entry when you press
       RETURN; it does not have to be at the end.

   Source: Lotus manual page 7

       The longer and more complicated the expression
in the cell, the more valuable is the edit mode.

Type B and C Problems

Type B and C problems expand your usage of Lotus' power and allow you to use formulas and relationships of cells. You will now specify relationships based upon your knowledge of the subject matter and certain spreadsheet design criteria.

(1) Type B problems guide your selection of number inser-
     tion with the same code '# NA'. Also the insertion of
     a formula is indicated by a '=NA'. This provides you
     with some guidance. Problems 2, 3, and 4 are type B
     problems.

(2) Type C problems require formula and number insertions
     as well. However, type C templates do not provide
     guidance as to when to input a number or formula.

Entering formulas: a few hints

(1) Begin and end formulas with parentheses. This alerts
     Lotus that the input is a value and not a label.
     For example, if you wanted to multiply cell A1 by cell
     A2, by typing "A1*A2", Lotus would interpret the "A"
     as a label and would tell you that the command was
     impossible.
         A value is a number or a formula.
         A label is any entry that is not a number or a
         formula as determined by Lotus. Lotus regards
         anything, even a number, preceded by an
         apostrophe,', as a label.
(2) Use cell locations as a factor in your formulas
     whenever possible.

     example: 'B12' represents sales dollars of 100,000.
               You wish to enter a value of 'B13' for sales
               commissions--which is 10 percent of sales.
               Enter (B12*.10) as opposed to (100,000*
               .10). This allows you to make a future
               change of sales in only the first cell
               'B12'. Since 'B13' is a function of 'B12'
               you need no further entry.

(3) Use additional parentheses as necessary to indicate
     the order of calculation.

     example: (12*(C15/2))

               C15 will first be divided by 2, then
               multiplied by 12.

9

or

((12*C15)/2)

C15 will be multipled by 12 first, then
divided by 2.

(4) Do not make reference to an undefined cell

(i.e. (N106*M11)--if you have no value in N106).

(5) Summary of algebraic Lotus symbols:
* (multiplication)
/ (division)
+ (addition)
- (subtraction)

5. Printing a solution

All templates in this workbook have been designed to print
on 8 1/2 inch paper. We are using only a small portion of
Lotus' grid which extends to 256 columns. Release 2 of Lotus
has a grid size of 8192 rows and 256 columns. You will become
very unpopular in the computer lab if you attempt to print the
entire Lotus grid.

First make sure the cursor is at A1. (This anchors the top
and left sides of the window to be printed.)

Then type:

/ P	(or move --> to Print and press Return)
P	(or move --> to Printer and press Return)
R	(or Return as cursor was on Range)
.	(to anchor the upper left corner to be 'painted' on the screen and printed)
->->	(to lower right cell used)

What you have done is to indicate the box that
you wish to be printed with A1 being your top
and left coordinate and pointing to the lower
right cell.

Return

G (or move --> to Go)

After printing your solution press P to allow the printer
to finish the page. The printer will then be set to begin
printing at the top of the next page. Then press Q to quit the
print mode and return to the spreadsheet.

Now continue the problem with any other changes indicated.
Then print the new solutions based on the new factors.

6. Printing Formulas

When you finish all solutions and printing of solutions for each problem, finish with one printout of formulas per problem.

Use the following commands.

/P (Print)
 P (Printer)
 O (Options)
 O (Other)
 C (Cell-Formulas)
 Q (Quit)
 G (Go)

Press P to finish the page and again line up the printer for its next job. If you are finished printing formulas you must tell Lotus to return to the usual template format when it next prints. The following commands will accomplish this task.

Q (Quit) this quits the print mode if you have not already
 /P (Print)
 P (Printer)
 O (Options)
 O (Other)
 A (As-displayed)
 Q (Quit)

7. Clearing the Screen to begin again or select another problem

/ F (File)
 R (Retrieve)

8. Saving a Solution

The following instruction will assist you in saving a solution. You may want to save a solution if the lab is about to close, class is about to begin, etc. The write-protect tab must first be removed from your disk (the little tab on the upper right). This will allow you to write to your disk. When you next use Lotus, simply retrieve your solution and finish the problem.

/	This is the command prompt
F	(File)
S	(Save)
new name	Type sol1a (for solution 1 a) or a similar code such that you create a new file rather than saving over and losing the existing file. (Your names may be up to 8 characters long, but may not include spaces or any other characters except A through Z, or 0 through 9.

9. Exiting Lotus

If you are in the print mode:

Q   (Quits the print mode)

Then use the following commands if you are on the spreadsheet:

/	(Puts you in the command mode)
Q	(Quit the spreadsheet)
Y	(Yes you want to quit)
E	(Exit Lotus 1-2-3)
Y	(Yes you want to exit Lotus 1-2-3)

When the disk drive lights go out remove disks and turn off machine.

10. Copying Cells or Ranges of Cells

Purpose: To eliminate the retyping of information already existing in a cell or range of cells.

Instructions: First put the cursor on the cell that you are copying from. The appropriate commands follow:

/	(Brings up the command menu)
C	(copy)

Copy from: Return   (if you want to copy only this cell as opposed to a range of cells)
               or
                         (to anchor this cell as the first cell of a desired range from which you want to copy)
               ->   (point, with the appropriate arrow key or keys to the last cell that you wish to copy from)

               Return   (when the range you want is indicated)

Copy to: ->   (point, with the appropriate arrow key or keys to the first cell that you wish to copy to)
               Return   (if you are copying only to one cell)
                         (Note: you can only copy a cell to a cell and not a range to a cell)
               or
               .   (to anchor this cell as the first cell of a range that you are copying to)
                         (Note: you can copy a range to a range or a cell to a range)
               ->   (point, with the appropriate arrow key or keys to the last cell that you wish to copy to)
               Return   (when the range you want is indicated)

Summary: You may copy: a cell to a cell
                           a cell to a range
                           a range to a range
          You may not copy: a range to a cell

Note: Lotus will assume a relative copy is desired as opposed to an absolute copy.

	A	B	C	D	E
1		January	February	March	Total
2					
3	Sales	1000	1500	1550	4050
4	Cost of sales	400	840	850	2090
5	Gross profit	(b3-b4)	?	?	?

In this case you may desire to copy the relationship of sales minus cost of sales to get gross profit to c5,d5 and e5. Lotus will automatically adjust for the different column locations. (i.e. c5 will become (c3-c4) and not the value of

13

(b3-b4). Consequently, what you have copied (and what you will be frequently copying) is a relationship as opposed to an absolute number or value. Be sure that the area to which you are copying is blank, or Lotus will overwrite whatever is there.

11. Summing: The @sum function

Purpose: To sum a range of cells without having to type every cell you wish to add.

Instructions: If you wish to add the values in cells c6 through c14, type the following:

@sum(c6.c14)

It sure beats having to type:

(c6+c7+c8+c9+c10+c11+c12+c13+c14)

Get in the habit of using this one frequently as well as the copy command as they will save you much time and energy (and impress your friends).

12. Making comparisons: The @if function

Purpose: The @if function can work effectively as a check for logic in your spreadsheet or for making comparisons.

Instructions: (An example is worth a thousand words.)

@if(B6>B7,B7,0)

In this case if the value in B6 is greater than the value in B7 then the value in B7 will be generated in this cell, otherwise 0 will result. The logic is summarized below:

@if(condition,value if true,value if false)

Problem ten applies the @if function.

13. Template Design Procedures and Policy

There are certain design procedures and general policies which encourage the proper use of spreadsheets in practice. Accountants are often key figures in developing and implementing these plans. The next section discusses these issues. You will note that we have applied some of these procedures to the templates in this workbook.

14

Control Plans to Encourage Proper Use of Spreadsheets

We would like to be sure that the spreadsheet logic accurately reflects what the designer intended, that the logic used by the designer is appropriate to the problem, and that the data used in the model is accurate. These goals can can be difficult to achieve, either in the laboratory or in actual practice.

It is quite feasible to construct a spreadsheet which works without error but implements a logic not appropriate to the problem. There will be no error signal from the program for this type of error. The discovery of this type depends on two factors; a detailed understanding of the process being modeled, and a quality review process of the model as constructed.

Control plans to assure proper logic include assigning personnel with both technical spreadsheet skills, and the knowledge of the particular problem to the development of the spreadsheet; require that the spreadsheets be tested with known data, calculated manually; record the history of the development and testing of the spreadsheet in a "documentation" area on the spreadsheet.

Another threat to the proper use of spreadsheets in practice is the informal sharing of spreadsheets which occurs in organizations. Users borrow spreadsheets from others, and apply them without adequately examining the quality of the spreadsheet itself or its appropriateness to their own particular use.

The control plan to meet this threat is to route models through a quality control center which can aid in the dissemination of the model to all those who may be able to use it. The quality control center can also assess the appropriateness of the model for the potential new use. Many firms have instituted these quality control centers.

A paper record of the spreadsheet logic should always be available. This aids in performing the quality review mentioned above and aids a user in answering questions about the spreadsheet. A new printout should be run whenever the spreadsheet is revised. Whenever you construct or complete a template in this set, you are required to print a set of formulas.

Lotus only prints the formulas in a verticle column by consecutive spreadsheet address. You will see that this is a difficult format to use in reviewing your spreadsheet. The Sreadsheet Auditor, a program which works in conjunction with Lotus, will print formulas and the value of each cell based on current data in the model. The format used by the Spreadsheet

Auditor is the same as that of the worksheet. The Spreadsheet
Auditor will also perform certain other tests on the
spreadsheet to help detect errors.

Thus, control plans to require proper use of spreadsheet
logic, and to use a program like The Spreadsheet Auditor in the
quality review process help assure the proper use of the
electronic spreadsheet.

The accuracy of data input is a major obstacle to the
proper use of spreadsheets. If the construction of spreadsheet
logic is sometimes an ad-hoc procedure, data input procedures
are even more so. Often, data input personnel are not the same
persons who designed the spreadsheet, having less familiarity
with spreadsheets and less knowledge of the model. On the
other hand, spreadsheet designers sometimes do not design
efficient data entry sections on the worksheet to aid data
entry personnel.

Some of the same control plans both encourage accuracy of
data input and protect the spreadsheet logic. The principal
control plan is to separate the data entry section of the
worksheet from the logic section. Once this separation is
accomplished, there are three other steps to take. First,
design the data input section to resemble forms familiar to
data entry personnel. Professionally designed forms are
arranged in logical order, and encourage economy of keystrokes.
Second, establish a policy which prohibits data entry personnel
from using any other part of the spreadsheet. Lotus has an
electronic cell protection feature which may also be utilized,
but it is easily overridden. Third, make all references from
the logic section of the worksheet to the data entry section of
the worksheet, refer to cell addresses rather than to the value
in a cell. Referencing cell addresses means that once the data
is changed in the data section, then the logic section
automatically calculates new results. You will greatly
appreciate this feature in doing several iterations of a
spreadsheet with different data.

Illustration of a Spreadsheet

The following figure illustrates some of the control plans
discussed above. Each figure is annotated. Study the
illustrations, and refer back to the discussion of control
plans as needed.

*This figure was taken from the May, 1986, issue of the Journal
of Accountancy, copyright ⓒ 1986 by the American Institute of
Certified Public Accountants.

A spreadsheet for analyzing
the cash flow implications of purchasing an automobile

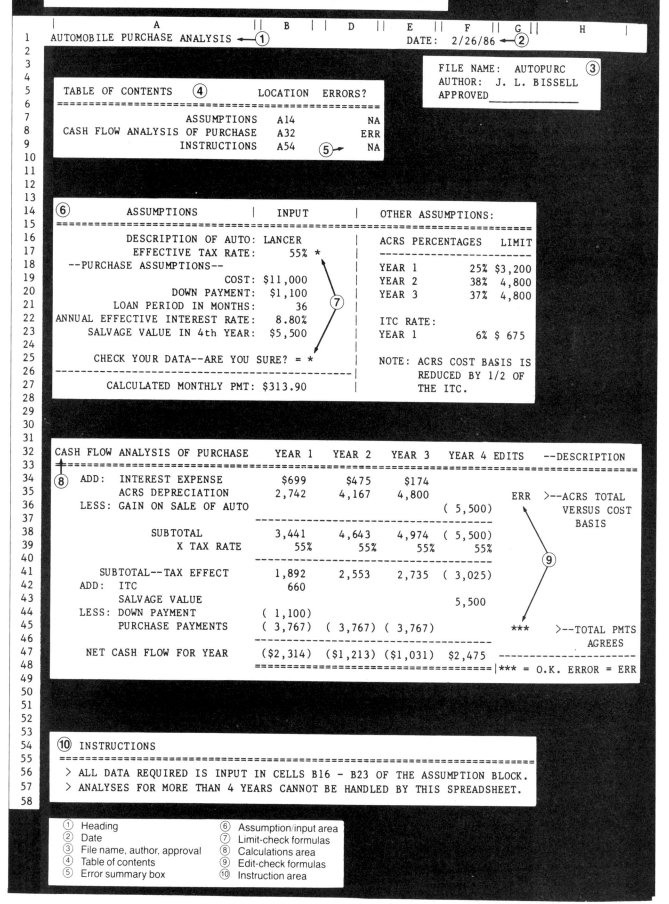

```
     |              A              ||  B  | |   D   || E ||  F   || G ||      H       |
 1   AUTOMOBILE PURCHASE ANALYSIS ←①                   DATE:  2/26/86 ←②
 2
 3                                                        FILE NAME:  AUTOPURC    ③
 4                                                        AUTHOR:  J. L. BISSELL
 5   TABLE OF CONTENTS    ④          LOCATION  ERRORS?    APPROVED _____
 6   ================================================
 7                          ASSUMPTIONS    A14           NA
 8   CASH FLOW ANALYSIS OF PURCHASE    A32               ERR
 9                         INSTRUCTIONS    A54            NA
10                                     ⑤→
11
12
13
14   ⑥       ASSUMPTIONS      |  INPUT  |   OTHER ASSUMPTIONS:
15   ==================================================================
16         DESCRIPTION OF AUTO: LANCER    |  ACRS PERCENTAGES   LIMIT
17           EFFECTIVE TAX RATE:    55% *  |  -----------------------
18     --PURCHASE ASSUMPTIONS--            |  YEAR 1        25% $3,200
19                     COST: $11,000       |  YEAR 2        38%  4,800
20            DOWN PAYMENT:  $1,100        |  YEAR 3        37%  4,800
21      LOAN PERIOD IN MONTHS:    36   ⑦   |
22   ANNUAL EFFECTIVE INTEREST RATE: 8.80% |  ITC RATE:
23     SALVAGE VALUE IN 4th YEAR: $5,500   |  YEAR 1         6% $ 675
24                                         |
25     CHECK YOUR DATA--ARE YOU SURE? = *  |  NOTE: ACRS COST BASIS IS
26   --------------------------------------|        REDUCED BY 1/2 OF
27       CALCULATED MONTHLY PMT: $313.90   |        THE ITC.
28
29
30
31
32   CASH FLOW ANALYSIS OF PURCHASE   YEAR 1   YEAR 2   YEAR 3   YEAR 4 EDITS  --DESCRIPTION
33   ================================================================================
34   ⑧  ADD:   INTEREST EXPENSE       $699     $475     $174
35            ACRS DEPRECIATION      2,742    4,167    4,800
36      LESS: GAIN ON SALE OF AUTO                      ( 5,500)   ERR  >--ACRS TOTAL
37                                  ----------------------------             VERSUS COST
38            SUBTOTAL              3,441    4,643    4,974  ( 5,500)         BASIS
39            X TAX RATE             55%      55%      55%      55%
40                                  ----------------------------      ⑨
41        SUBTOTAL--TAX EFFECT       1,892    2,553    2,735  ( 3,025)
42   ADD:  ITC                        660
43         SALVAGE VALUE                                       5,500
44   LESS: DOWN PAYMENT            ( 1,100)
45         PURCHASE PAYMENTS       ( 3,767) ( 3,767) ( 3,767)        ***  >--TOTAL PMTS
46                                  ----------------------------             AGREES
47   NET CASH FLOW FOR YEAR       ($2,314) ($1,213) ($1,031)  $2,475  ----------------------
48                                ================================|*** = O.K. ERROR = ERR
49
50
51
52
53
54   ⑩  INSTRUCTIONS
55   ================================================================================
56    > ALL DATA REQUIRED IS INPUT IN CELLS B16 - B23 OF THE ASSUMPTION BLOCK.
57    > ANALYSES FOR MORE THAN 4 YEARS CANNOT BE HANDLED BY THIS SPREADSHEET.
58
```

① Heading   ⑥ Assumption/input area
② Date   ⑦ Limit-check formulas
③ File name, author, approval   ⑧ Calculations area
④ Table of contents   ⑨ Edit-check formulas
⑤ Error summary box   ⑩ Instruction area

Summary

We have discussed why spreadsheete are important from the point of view of an accounting student. You have an abbreviated set of instructions for the use of Lotus. These instructions will provide you with the fundamentals of spreadsheet use. You will find your facility increasing greatly as you solve more problems. Finally, we discussed the problems encountered in using spreadsheets in practice. Control plans were recommended to solve or at least control these problems.

One last tip. Proper preparation before entering the computer lab is most important. Remember, you are responsible for both the technical accounting knowledge, and the proper use of the spreadsheet. Be sure you have command over the problem material. Keep notes on what you learn in succeeding lab sessions. Have a plan which you are ready to apply in the lab. It makes sense to sketch out your plan on paper before entering the lab. The format we use for problem presentation shows the outline of the template with rows and columns labelled. You can use this to draft your plan. Good luck!

References

Bromley, Robert G., "Template Design and Review: How to Prevent Spreadsheet Disasters," Journal of Accountancy (December, 1985) pp. 134-142.

Howit, Doran, "Avoiding Bottom-Line Disaster," Infoworld (February 11, 1985) pp. 26-30.

Lotus Development Corp., Lotus 123, Release 1A, Lotus Development Corp., Cambridge, Ma. 1983.

Maremaa, Tom, "1-2-3 Add-Ons Find a Ready Market," Infoworld (July 8, 1985) pp. 30-32.

McCarthy, Michael, "Getting the Most Out of Your Spreadsheet," Personal Computing (June, 1984) pp. 136-149.

Software Digest, Inc, "How Do Spreadsheet Programs Compare?" Journal of Accountancy (December, 1985) pp.142-145.

Waller, Thomas C. and Gallun, Rebecca A., "Microcomputer Literacy Requirements in the Accounting Industry," Journal of Accounting Education (Vol.3, No.2, Fall, 1985)

(There are a host of articles and "how to" books written about spreadsheets. In addition, one of the best ways to learn about these tools is to read detailed product testing reports conducted by various independent magazines. Software Digest, Inc. publishes a newsletter for various types of software, including spreadsheets. Your work with spreadsheets will give you a real feel for the issues involved.)

PROBLEM 1   CONTRIBUTION MARGIN STATEMENTS, TAXES

Case	Unit Selling Price	Unit Variable Cost	Fixed Costs	Unit Sales
1.	$ 16	$ 10	$ 4,000	2,000
2.	20	14	36,000	9,000
3.	30	22	220,000	31,000
4.	13	8	115,000	27,000

Required:

1. Prepare income statements for each case shown, assuming a
    40% income tax rate.

2. Determine the sales, in units, required to double the
    after-tax income that you computed for each situation.

3. Prepare income statements for each case shown, assuming a 45%
    income tax rate.

4. What are the advantages and disadvantages of an analysis
    such as 2. above, using after-tax income as opposed to pre-
    tax income? (Answer on a separate sheet of paper.)

Notes to students: This is a Type A problem. You only have to
insert values in the Data Section.   Notice how formulas have
already been entered for you in the Logic Section.   You can
examine the individual formulas by placing the curser on cells you
are interested in.   The formulas are indicated on the upper
left corner of the screen.

	A	B	C	D	E	F	G	H
1	PROBLEM ONE CONTRIBUTION MARGIN STATEMENTS, TAXES							
2	TYPE: A							
3								
4	NAME: _____							
5	DATE: _____							
6								
7	Data Section-(Use values in this section of a spreadsheet.)							
8				(1)	(2)	(3)	(4)	
9								
10	Unit Sales			# NA	#NA	#NA	# NA	
11	Unit Selling Price			# NA	#NA	#NA	# NA	
12	Unit Variable Cost			# NA	#NA	#NA	# NA	
13	Total Fixed Costs			# NA	#NA	#NA	# NA	
14	Tax Rate (enter decimal)			# NA	#NA	#NA	# NA	
15								
16	Place an 'X' after the requirement you are solving.							
17	Requirement 1: _____							
18	Requirement 3: _____							
19								
20	Logic Section (Use cell referencing from the Data Section and							

	A	B	C	D	E	F	G	H
21			formulas in this section of a spreadsheet.)					
22								
23	Sales			NA	NA	NA	NA	
24	Variable Costs			NA	NA	NA	NA	
25								
26	Contribution Margin			NA	NA	NA	NA	
27	Fixed Costs			NA	NA	NA	NA	
28								
29	Income Before Taxes			NA	NA	NA	NA	
30	Income Taxes @ 40%			NA	NA	NA	NA	
31								
32	Net Income			NA	NA	NA	NA	
33								
34								
35	Requirement 2							
36			Required	+	=	(/)	=	
37		Old N.I.	Pretax	Fixed	Required	C.M.	Required	
38	Case	x 2	Profit*	Costs	C.M.	per unit	Sales	
39								
40								
41	1.	NA	NA	NA	NA	# NA	NA	
42	2.	NA	NA	NA	NA	# NA	NA	
43	3.	NA	NA	NA	NA	# NA	NA	
44	4.	NA	NA	NA	NA	# NA	NA	
45								
46	*When divided by 60% = (1 - tax rate).							

PROBLEM 2 VCP ANALYSIS-PRODUCT MIX

Happy Times Brewery produces and sells two grades of beer; regular and premium. Premium beer sells for $6.50 per case, regular for $4.25. Variable brewing costs per case are $3.10 (premium) and $2.05 (regular). Sales of regular beer, in cases, are double those for premium. Fixed brewing costs are $90,000 monthly, and fixed selling and administrative costs are $75,000 monthly. The only variable cost in addition to variable brewing costs is 10% commission (based on dollar sales) paid to salespeople.

Required:

1. Compute the break-even point in cases and dollars per month.
2. Compute the above calculations assuming the following projections:
   a) Premium beer sells for $6.80 per case.
   b) Regular beer sells for $4.10 per case.
   c) Sales projections indicate that for every case of premium beer sold three cases of regular beer will be sold.
   d) All other information is the same.
3. Compute the above calculations assuming the following projections:
   a) Premium beer sells for $6.25 per case.
   b) Regular beer sells for $4.40 per case.
   c) Sales projections indicate that for every two cases of premium beer sold, three cases of regular beer will be sold.
4. Which pricing structure would you recommend and why? (Answer on separate sheet of paper.)

Notes to students: This is a Type A problem. You are required to enter only values in the Data Section. Note how the Logic Section already contains formulas and consequently solves the problem for you as you fill in the data.

```
        A       B      C        D         E          F          G          H
1   PROBLEM TWO   VCP ANALYSIS-PRODUCT MIX
2   TYPE: A
3
4   NAME: _____
5   DATE: _____
6
7   Place an 'X' after the requirement you are solving.
8       Requirement 1: _____
9       Requirement 2: _____
10      Requirement 3: _____
11
12  Data Section
13                                  S.P.       Var.
14                          Sales   Per     S. Com.    Var.
15                          Ratio*  Unit       %       Brew.
16
17  Reg. Beer               # NA    # NA      # NA      #NA
18  Prem. Beer              # NA    # NA      # NA      #NA
19  * i.e. '1' Reg. to '1' Prem. etc.
20
        A       B      C        D         E          F          G          H          I
21  Fixed Costs:
22
23  Brewing       #NA
24  Selling & A   #NA
25  Other         #NA
26
27  Logic Section
28
29                  S.P.    Total       Var.     Net      Var.     Total Var   C.M.
30          Sales Per   Sales Per   Sales    Sales    Brewing   Brewing    Per
31          Ratio Unit  Ratio       Comm.  After Com  Per Unit   /Ratio    Ratio
32
33  Reg     NA    NA      NA          NA       NA        NA         NA        NA
34  Prem    NA    NA      NA          NA       NA        NA         NA        NA
35                      _____   _____  _____  _____  _____  _____
36
37          Totals      NA          NA       NA        NA         NA        NA
38
39
40  Contribution Margin Per Composite Unit: =>        NA
41
42  Total Fixed Costs: = >                            NA
43
44  Break-even Point For Composite Unit: =>           NA
45
46
47                      In              In Sales
48                      Units           Dollars
49                      _____           _____
50
51  Regular Beer        NA              NA
52  Premium Beer        NA              NA
53                      _____        _____
54  Total               NA              NA
55                      _____        _____
56                      _____        _____
57
```

PROBLEM 3   PRODUCT LINE REPORTING

The Kelly Company is a retail store specializing in men's clothing. The firm's most recent monthly income statement is given below:

Sales		$800,000
Cost of Sales		572,000
Gross Profit		228,000
Operating Expenses:		
Commissions	$48,000	
Salaries	80,000	
Rent	20,000	
Shipping & Delivery	15,000	
Insurance	4,500	
Miscellaneous	7,500	175,000
Income before taxes		$ 53,000

The president of the firm would like a product line income statement. She gives you the following additional data:

1. The sales mix in April was 30% suits, 50% sport clothes, and 20% accessories, expressed in dollars of total sales.
2. The cost of sales percentages are 80% for suits, 75% for sport clothes, and 50% for accessories.
3. Sales commissions are 6% for all product lines.
4. Each product line is the responsibility of a separate manager and each manager has a small staff. The salaries that are directly related to each product line are $12,000 for suits, $8,000 for sport clothes, and $5,200 for accessories. All other salaries are joint to the three lines.
5. Rent is for the office and warehouse space, all of which is in a single building.
6. Shipping and delivery costs are for operating expenses and depreciation on the firm's three trucks, including drivers' salaries. Each truck serves a particular geographical area and delivers all three products.
7. Insurance includes a $500 fixed amount for basic liability coverage. The rest of the insurance is for coverage of merchandise at the rate of one-half of one percent of the selling price of the average inventory on hand during the month. In April the average inventories at selling prices were equal to sales for each product line.
8. Miscellaneous expenses are all joint to the three product lines.

Required:

1. Prepare an income statement by product.
2. Compute the above considering the following changes: the sales mix was 35% suits, 55% sport clothes and 10%

23

accessories. The cost of sales percentages are 75% for suits, 70% for sport clothes and 60% for accessories. All other information is the same as above.

3. Compute the above considering the following changes: the sales mix was 25% suits, 55% sport clothes and 20% accessories. The cost of sales percentages are 85% for suits, 70% for suits, and 40% for accessories. All other information is the same as above.

4. What can you conclude about a desired sales mix? (Answer on a separate sheet of paper.)

Notes to students: This is a Type B problem. The Data Section is partially complete and needs completion by you. Additionally, you must fill in the formulas for the Logic Section. We see several opportunities for use of the Copy function in the successful completion of the Logic Section of this problem. Refer to the front material in this supplement for instruction on the Copy function.

   If you are feeling brave, consider cell G49. It would be helpful here to check your logic and see if the sum of the product margins is equal to the sales less costs in the Total column. A logic function could serve this purpose. Refer again to the front material in this supplement for details on the logic function, the '@if' function. Try entering this in cell H49:

$$@if(@sum(D49.F49)=(G37-G43-G47),0,99999)$$

This says that if the sum of the product margins is equal to the total sales less costs then a '0' will be printed in cell H49. If for some reason this is not true a '99999' will be printed in cell H49. For your own purposes in using spreadsheets you might like this kind of check. Using a default of '99999' alerts you to the fact that your spreadsheet is not working. This type of logic function we find very helpful. Our only caution in your personal use of this type of function is to beware of Lotus' precision. A slight rounding difference could send this function into default - resulting in a '99999'. You can overcome this problem by either a Global rounding function for the entire spreadsheet (which you can read about in your Lotus manual) or by restating this logic function to read: the rounded sum of the product margins is equal to the rounded difference of the total sales less costs. Good luck!

```
         A         B         C         D         E         F         G         H
1   PROBLEM THREE   PRODUCT LINE REPORTING
2   TYPE: B
3
4   NAME:        _ _ _ _ _ _
5   DATE:        _ _ _ _ _ _ _ _
6
7   Place an 'X' after the requirement you are solving.
8       Requirement 1:    _ _ _ _ _ _ _ _
9       Requirement 2:    _ _ _ _ _ _ _ _
10      Requirement 3:    _ _ _ _ _ _ _ _
11
12  Data Section
13
14                        Suits    S-Coats   Access.    Total
15  Sales Total                                                  NA
16  Sales Mix % *           NA        NA        NA
17  COS % *                 NA        NA        NA
18  Sales Com. % *          NA        NA        NA
19  Sales Salaries          NA        NA        NA
20  Joint Salaries                                               NA


         A         B         C         D         E         F         G         H
21  Rent                                                         NA
22  Ship. & Del.                                                 NA
23  Insurance (Fixed)                                            NA
24  Var. Ins. -
25    (% of Inv.)*          NA        NA        NA
26  Misc.                                                        NA
27    *Please insert decimal.
```

	A	B	C	D	E	F	G	H
28								
29								
30					Kelly Company			
31				Product Line Income Statement For April 19x7				
32								
33					Sports	Acces-		
34				Suits	Clothes	sories	Total	
35				------	--------	------	-----	
36								
37	Sales			NA	NA	NA	NA	
38	Variable Costs:							
39	Cost of Sales			NA	NA	NA	NA	
40	Commissions (6% of sales)			NA	NA	NA	NA	

	A	B	C	D	E	F	G	H
41	Insurance			NA	NA	NA	NA	
42				---------------------------------------				
43	Total Variable Costs			NA	NA	NA	NA	
44				---------------------------------------				
45	Contribution Margin			NA	NA	NA	NA	
46	Separable Discretionary							
47	Fixed Costs: Salaries			NA	NA	NA	NA	
48				---------------------------------------				
49	Product Margin			NA	NA	NA	NA	
50				---------------------------------------				
51	Joint and Committed							
52	Fixed Costs:							
53	Salaries						NA	
54	Rent						NA	
55	Shipping and Delivery						NA	
56	Insurance						NA	
57	Miscellaneous						NA	
58	Total Joint and Committed Costs						NA	
59							---------	
60	Income						NA	
61							--------	
62							--------	
63								

PROBLEM 4   PRODUCT LINE INCOME STATEMENTS

The president of the Mifflan Tool Company has just received the firm's income statement for January 19X8. He is puzzled because you had told him last year, when working as a consultant to the firm, that sales of $500,000 should produce a profit of about $57,000 before income taxes.

Mifflan Tool Company
Income Statement
January 19X8

Sales		$500,000
Cost of sales		307,500
Gross profit		192,500
Operating expenses:		
Rent	$40,000	
Salaries	70,000	
Shipping & Del.	14,000	
Other expenses	30,000	154,000
Income before taxes		$ 38,500

The firm sells three products and your analysis assumed the following sales mix in dollars: hammers, 30%; screwdrivers, 20%; and chisels, 50%. The actual mix in dollars in January was 40%, 30%, 30%. The firm does not manufacture its products. Cost of sales and shipping and delivery are variable costs. All others are fixed. Data per unit for each product are given below:

	Hammers	Screwdrivers	Chisels
Selling price	$5.00	$2.00	$4.00
Cost of sales	3.00	1.50	2.00
Shipping and delivery	.20	.04	.08
Total variable costs	3.20	1.54	2.08
Contribution margin	$1.80	$ .46	$1.92

None of the fixed costs is directly associated with any particular product line. All costs were incurred as expected, per unit for variable costs, total for fixed costs. Selling prices were as expected.

Required:
1. Prepare an income statement by product, based on actual results in January. Show both gross profit and contribution margin for each product.
2. Prepare an income statement by product for January, assuming that the expected sales mix had been achieved.
3. An alternative manufacturing process would alter the cost structure in the following manner. First, cost of sales per unit would be Hammers-$3.10; Screwdrivers-$1.55; and Chisels-$2.05.   These increases in variable costs are a result of a decrease in other expenses to $25,000.   Other information is the same. Complete requirement 2 from above assuming these changes.
4. Alternatively other expenses may increase to $37,000.   This would result in a decrease in cost of sales to: Hammers-$2.85;

Screwdrivers-$1.40; and Chisels-$1.85. All other information is the same. Using these assumptions solve requirement 2 above.

	A	B	C	D	E	F	G	H
1	PROBLEM FOUR PRODUCT LINE INCOME STATEMENTS							
2	TYPE: C							
3								
4	NAME:		NA					
5	DATE:		NA					
6								
7	Place an 'X' after the requirement you are solving.							
8	Requirement 1:		_____					
9	Requirement 2:		_____					
10	Requirement 3:		_____					
11	Requirement 4:		_____					
12								
13	Data Section							
14				Hammers	Drivers	Chisels	Total	
15	Total Sales						NA	
16	Sales mix in percentages*			NA	NA	NA		
17	Selling Price per unit			NA	NA	NA		
18	Cost of Sales per unit			NA	NA	NA		
19	Ship. & Del. per unit			NA	NA	NA		
20	Fixed costs:							

	A	B	C	D	E	F	G	H
21	Rent						NA	
22	Salaries						NA	
23	Other Expenses						NA	
24	*Please insert decimal.							
25								
26	Logic Section							
27								
28								
29				Mifflan Company				
30				Income Statement				
31								
32				Hammers	Drivers	Chisels	Totals	
33				---				
34								
35	Sales							
36	Cost of Sales							
37				_____	_____	_____	_____	
38	Gross Profit							
39	Shipping and Delivery							
40				_____	_____	_____	_____	

	A	B	C	D	E	F	G	H
41	Contribution Margin							
42	Fixed Costs							
43				_____	_____	_____	_____	
44	Income before Taxes							
45								
46				_____	_____	_____	_____	
47				_____	_____	_____	_____	
48								

PROBLEM 5   JOINT PRODUCTS

TAB Company produces four joint products at a joint cost of $80,000. All products are currently processed beyond the split-off point, and the final products are sold as follows,

Products	Sales	Additional Processing Costs
M	$160,000	$120,000
N	180,000	60,000
O	45,000	40,000
P	30,000	25,000

The firm could sell the products at the split-off point for the following amounts: M, $80,000; N, $50,000; O, $15,000; and P, zero.

Required:

1. Determine which products the firm should sell at the split-off point.

2. Determine what TAB's profit would be if it took the most profitable action with respect to each of its products.

3. Determine which products the firm should sell at the split-off point if the following additional processing costs are incurred. (All other information remains unchanged.)

	Addition Processing Costs:
M	$ 65,000
N	120,000
O	25,000
P	21,000

4. In general, what can you conclude about decisions involving the further processing of products? Please answer on a separate sheet of paper.

Notes to students:
1. Take a look at cell D37. In this cell you are looking for the sales value resulting from the optimal decision of whether to sell at split-off or process further. The '@if' function allows you to use spreadsheet logic to determine the appropriate sales figure. The formula: @if(D33>0,D26,D27) is given for you. Refer to the front material in your supplement for a discussion of the @if function. This formula says that if further processing of M results in a gain (i.e.>0 in cell D33) then the further processing revenue will be printed. If the condition is false then the appropriate sales figure is the split-off sales (i.e. D27). Your task is to create the appropriate logic functions for cells E37-G37 using similar logic.
2. Cell D38 requires a processing cost if the product is further processed. Analyze the formula given in D38. Produce similar formulas for E38 - G38.

```
         A         B          C          D          E          F          G          H
1  PROBLEM FIVE   JOINT PRODUCTS
2  TYPE: B
3
4  NAME:        _____
5  DATE:        _____
6
7  Data Section
8                                         M          N          O          P          Total
9  Sales Value:
10   @ split-off                          NA         NA         NA         NA
11   if further processed                 NA         NA         NA         NA
12 Costs:
13   further processing                   NA         NA         NA         NA
14   joint                                                                            NA
15
16 Logic Section
17
18
19                                                            Product
20  1.        _____

         A         B          C          D          E          F          G          H
21                                         M          N          O          P          Total
22           _____
23
24
25 Marginal Revenue:
26   If processed further                 NA         NA         NA         NA         NA
27   If sold at split off                 NA         NA         NA         NA         NA
28           _____
29   Marginal revenue                     NA         NA         NA         NA         NA
30   Marginal costs                       NA         NA         NA         NA         NA
31           _____
32 Gain (loss) from further
33   processing                           NA         NA         NA         NA         NA
34           _____
35
36  2.
37 Sales                                  NA         NA         NA         NA         NA
38 Additional processing costs            NA         NA         NA         NA         NA
39           _____
40 Margin                                 NA         NA         NA         NA         NA

         A         B          C          D          E          F          G          H
41 Joint Costs                                                                        NA
42                                                                                    _____
43 Profit                                                                             NA
44                                                                                    _____
45                                                                                    _____
46
47
```

Marie Angelo, the owner of Gino's Pizzeria, is considering the possibility of introducing a "luncheon special" to increase business during the slow time from 11:00 A.M. to 1:00 P.M. on weekdays. For $2.20 on any weekday, she will give a customer all the pizza he or she can eat. Marie has prepared the following data for current business during those hours for a one-week period:

	Pizza	Beverages	Total
Sales (ave. pizza price,$2.80)	$420	$84	$504
Variable costs	120	24	144
Contribution margin	300	60	360
Avoidable fixed costs-			
wages of students hired			180
Current incremental profit,lunch			$180

She estimates that if she offers the special price, she will be serving about 300 pizzas per week to about 250 customers. (Some customers are expected to eat more than one pizza, given the lower price.) She also anticipates that variable costs per unit will be about 20% higher than they are now because people will want more toppings than they now order (pepperoni, sausage, hamburger, etc.). Beverage sales will bear the same relationship to the number of customers that they do now when each customer eats one pizza. The increase in the number of customers would entail an increase in personnel during the hours of the special, increasing costs by 15%.

Required:

1. Evaluate the monetary effects of the proposed "luncheon special".

2. A friend of Marie's suggested another luncheon special, the "cheapie luncheon special". For $1.50 a customer can eat all the cheese pizza he or she can eat. Variable costs on the average will fall 10% with this special as most people will be eating only cheese pizza. Beverage sales will remain the same as above. The increase in the number of customers will be similar to the above special. The increase in personnel during the hours of the special will be similar to the above special.

3. Are there any other critical factors that should be taken into account? If so, what are they? Answer on separate sheet of paper.

Notes to students: Have you noticed that there are no '$'s on these financial statements to date. Let's put some on. Examine the Data Section. The numbers in row 11 refer to unit sales, so lets not turn them into dollars. However, rows 12,13,14 and 15 all refer to dollars of sales or expenses. The commands to convert these numbers to currency are as follows:

```
/
R          (range)
F          (format)
C          (currency)
(Return)   (you are accepting currency)
C12.H15    (you are indicating which range)
(Return)   (you are accepting that range)
```

If this works, and it should, be brave and see if you can convert the values in the income statement to currency. Note you simply refer to a different range than the above range.

In future problems, feel free to change the format to currency when appropriate.

```
        A          B           C          D          E           F          G          H
1   PROBLEM SIX    PRODUCT PRICING-OFF PEAK HOURS
2   TYPE: B
3
4   NAME:        _____
5   DATE:        _____
6
7   Data Section
8
9                                New Plan                            Old Plan
10                       Pizza Beverages   Total          Pizza Beverages   Total
11  Unit Sales            NA      NA                       NA      NA
12  Sales Price/unit      NA      NA                       NA      NA
13  Var. Cost/unit        NA      NA                       NA      NA
14  Avoid. Fixed Cost                         NA                                NA
15
16
17  Logic Section
18
19
20                                           New Plan                      Effect on
        A          B           C          D          E          F          G          H
21                                        _____  Current    Total
22                                                                                  Profit
23                                         Pizza Beverages   Totals      Plan
                                          ------------------------------------------------
24  Sales:
25    Pizza                                  NA                NA         NA         NA
26    Beverages                                        NA     NA         NA         NA
27                                                           --------------------------------
28                                                            NA         NA         NA
29                                                           --------------------------------
30  Variable Costs:
31    Pizza                                  NA                NA         NA         NA
32    Beverages                                        NA     NA         NA         NA
33                                          --------------------------------------------
34      Total  Costs,
35        Variable                           NA       NA      NA         NA         NA
36                                          --------------------------------------------
37  Contribution Margin                      NA       NA      NA         NA         NA
38                                          --------------------------------------------
39  Discretionary Costs                      -------------------  NA     NA         NA
40                                                           --------------------------------
41  Net Incremental Profit
42    for Lunch Period                                        NA         NA         NA
43                                                           --------------------------------
44                                                           --------------------------------
```

34

PROBLEM 7 SPECIAL ORDER

Brike Company, which manufactures robes, has enough idle capacity available to accept a special order of 10,000 robes at $8 a robe. A predicted income statement for the year without this special order is as follows:

	Per Unit	Total
Sales	$12.50	$1,250,000
Manufacturing costs- variable	6.25	625,000
Manufacturing costs- fixed	1.75	175,000
Manufacturing costs- total	8.00	800,000
Gross profit	4.50	450,000
Selling expenses-variable	1.80	180,000
Selling expenses-fixed	1.45	145,000
Selling expenses-total	3.25	325,000
Operating income	$ 1.25	$ 125,000

Required:

1. Assuming no additional selling expenses, what would be the effect on operating income if the special order was accepted?

2. Alternatively, Brike Company could accept a special order for 11,000 robes @ $8.50 per robe. As stated in the previous alternative, no additional selling expenses would be incurred.

Notes to students: This problem is short and sweet but encompasses a built in logic check on idle capacity. The formula is given for you in D21. Your job is to fill in Data Section with values and fill in the Logic Section with '@if' functions.

```
         A         B         C         D         E         F         G         H
1   PROBLEM SEVEN   SPECIAL ORDER
2   TYPE B:
3
4   NAME:        _____
5   DATE:        _____
6
7   Data Section
8                           Per Unit    Total
9   Selling price(old)        NA
10  Var. Man. Costs           NA
11  Var. Sell. Exp.           NA
12  Fixed Man. Costs                     NA
13  Fixed Selling                        NA
14
15  Special Order Selling Price
16  Special Order Units                  NA
17  Idle Capacity Units                  NA
18
19  Logic Section
20
         A         B         C         D         E         F         G         H
21     Idle Capacity check              NA
22
23                       Partial Income Statement
24
25  Sales - special order*               NA
26  Var. Man. Costs                      NA
27                                   _____
28   C.M. - spec. order                  NA
29   (Inc. or (Decr.) in op.
30     income)
31  *Try a logic function for the proper sales figure. Refer to 'D21'
32   for assistance.
33
34
```

@ IT(D21=0,0,D16 $\neq$ D15)
      10,000   8

36

PROBLEM 8   MULTIPLE MATERIALS-MANUFACTURING FIRM

Williams Company, expects the following sales by month, in units, for the first eight months of 19x9.

Budgeted	Jan.	Feb.	March	April	May	June	July	Aug.
Sales	1,500	1,800	1,900	2,500	1,900	2,000	2,000	1,800

The company's one product, the Tow, requires two raw materials: Tics and Tacs. Each Tow requires three Tics and two Tacs. Williams follows the policy of having finished goods equal to 50% of budgeted sales for the following two months. Raw material inventories are maintained at 150% of budgeted production needs for the coming month. All inventories at December 31, 19x8, reflect these policies.

Required:

A.   1. Prepare a production budget for Tows for as many months as you can.
     2. Prepare purchases budgets for Tics and Tacs for as many months as you can.

B.   Assume the Williams Company alters its production process such that each Tow requires three Tacs and two Tics. Complete requirements 1 and 2 above noting this change in production.

C.   Alternatively, Williams may be able to produce a Tow using 2 1/2 Tics and 2 1/2 Tacs. Complete requirements 1 and 2 above noting this possible change in production.

D.   Refer to your three printouts and make some recommendations on production to the Williams Company. (Please answer on a separate sheet of paper.)

37

```
         A         B         C         D    E    F    G    H    I    J    K
1   PROBLEM EIGHT   MULTIPLE MATERIALS-MANUFACTURING FIRM
2   TYPE: B
3
4   NAME:      _____
5   DATE:      _____
6
7   Data Section
8                             JAN  FEB  MAR  APR  MAY  JUN JULY  AUG
9   Unit Sales                NA   NA   NA   NA   NA   NA   NA   NA
10  Tics per Tow*             NA   NA   NA   NA   NA   NA   NA   NA
11  Tacs per Tow              NA   NA   NA   NA   NA   NA   NA   NA
12  Fin. Good %**             NA   NA   NA   NA   NA   NA   NA   NA
13  Raw Mat. % of Prod.**     NA   NA   NA   NA   NA   NA   NA   NA
14
15
16  *Entering the same figure under each month allows you to easily
17   copy totals in the logic section below.  See supplement for
18   more detail.
19  **Please enter a decimal.
20

         A         B         C         D    E    F    G    H    I    J    K
21  Place an 'X' after the requirement you are solving.
22      Requirement A:   _____
23      Requirement B:   _____
24      Requirement C:   _____
25
26  Logic Section
27
28                                    Production Budget - Tows
29
30                            JAN  FEB  MAR  APR  MAY  JUN JULY  AUG
31                            ------------------------------------------------
32
33  Desired Ending Inventory  NA   NA   NA   NA   NA   NA
34  Expected Sales            NA   NA   NA   NA   NA   NA   NA   NA
35                            ------------------------------------
36  Required                  NA   NA   NA   NA   NA   NA
37  Beginning Inventory       NA   NA   NA   NA   NA   NA
38                            ------------------------------------
39  Production                NA   NA   NA   NA   NA   NA
40
```

```
        A          B          C          D      E      F      G      H      I      J      K
41
42
43                                            Purchases  budget  -  Tics
44
45                                      JAN    FEB    MAR    APR    MAY    JUN
46
47  Desired Ending Inventory            NA     NA     NA     NA     NA
48  Expected Use                        NA     NA     NA     NA     NA
49                                      ------------------------------------------
50  Required                            NA     NA     NA     NA     NA
51  Beginning Inventory                 NA     NA     NA     NA     NA
52                                      ------------------------------------------
53  Purchases                           NA     NA     NA     NA     NA
54
55
56
57                                            Purchases  budget  -  Tacs
58
59  Desired Ending Inventory            NA     NA     NA     NA     NA
60  Expected Use                        NA     NA     NA     NA     NA
61                                      ------------------------------------------
62  Required                            NA     NA     NA     NA     NA
63  Beginning Inventory                 NA     NA     NA     NA     NA
64                                      ------------------------------------------
65  Purchases                           NA     NA     NA     NA     NA
66
67
68
69
70
71
72
73
74
75
76
77
78
79
80
```

PROBLEM 9   BUDGETING FOR A HOSPITAL (AICPA adapted)

The administrator of Taylor Memorial Hospital, Dr. Gale, has asked for your assistance in preparing the budget for 19x7, which he must present at the next meeting of the hospital's board of trustees. The hospital obtains its revenues through two types of charges: charges for use of a hospital room and charges for use of the operating room. The use of the basic rooms depends on whether or not the patient undergoes surgery during the stay in the hospital. Estimated data as to the types of patients and the related room requirements for 19x7 are as follows:

Type of Patient	Total Expected	Average Stay in Days	Room Selection %'s		
			Private	Semi	Ward
Surgical	2,400	10	15%	75%	10%
Medical only	2,100	8	10%	60%	30%

Basic room charges are $50, $40, and $30 for private, semiprivate, and ward, respectively.

Charges for use of the operating room are a function of the length of the operation and the number of persons required to be involved in the operation. The charge is $0.15 per man-minute. (A 'man-minute' is one person for one minute; if an operation requires three persons for 40 minutes, there would be a charge for 120 man-minutes at $0.15 per man-minute, or $18.) Based on past experience, the following is a breakdown of the types of operations to be performed:

Type of Operation	Number of Operations	Ave. Number of Min. per Operation	Ave. Number of Persons Required
Minor	1,200	30	4
Major-abdominal	400	90	6
Major-other	800	120	8

Required:

A. 1. Prepare a schedule of budgeted revenues from room charges by type of patient and type of room.
   2. Prepare a schedule of budgeted revenues from operating room charges by type of operation.

B. Prepare the above analysis assuming that the type of patient shifts to 2,600 surgical and 1,900 medical. The same relationship of types of operations still exists with the new surgical patients.

C. What are the implications of this shift for planning purposes?

Notes to students: In the real world a picture is worth a thousand words or, in this case, certainly a revenue statement or two.   Let's help out the administrator and produce a bar chart

40

to indicate the sources of these revenues. First, save your
completed shpreadsheet. Then use the following commands to
produce a bar chart breaking down revenues from room charges.

```
    /
    G    (graph)
    T    (type)
    B    (bar)
    A    (range of data values)
  F44.H44
  (Return)
    X    (data range)
  L30.N30
  (Return)
    V    (view)
    V    (return to spreadsheet)
    O    (options)
    T    (titles)
    F    (first)
  SOURCES OF REVENUES
  (Return)
    T    (titles)
    S    (second)
  BY ROOM TYPE
  (Return)
    Q    (quit)
    V    (view)
    V    (to return to spreadsheet)
```

1-2-3 doesn't have a graph print option. Therefore, you
must first save your graph using the following commands:

```
    /
    G  (graph)
    S  (save)
    Graph1
```

You must then exit the 1-2-3 session and remove your 1-2-3
disk and use the PrintGraph Program to printout your graph. At
this point you will have to determine if your particular printer
is capable of printing out a graph. Ask your lab attendant.
Use the following commands to print your graph.
Insert your PrintGraph disk
P   (PrintGraph)
Arrow down and highlight your graph, Graph1.
Return
P   (print)

In future problems use similar commands to investigate Lotus'
graphics capabilities. It is to your professional advantage that
you become at ease with this type of graphics package. See if you
can produce a bar graph indicating revenues generated from
the different types   of operations.

```
          A         B         C         D         E         F         G         H
 1  PROBLEM NINE    BUDGETING FOR A HOSPITAL
 2  TYPE:   B
 3
 4  NAME:      _____
 5  DATE:      _____
 6
 7  Data Section
 8
 9  Type of              Total     Avg.      Total               Semi-
10  Patient              Expected  Stay      Days      Private   Private   Ward
11  ---------            --------------------------------------------------------
12  Surgical             NA        NA        NA        NA        NA        NA
13  Medical              NA        NA        NA        NA        NA        NA
14  --Room Rates                                       NA        NA        NA
15
16   Type      Avg. #    Avg. #    Avg. #       #      Total     Rate Per
17    Of        Of        Of       Of Man    Of Oper-  Man-      Man-
18  Operation Minutes   People    Minutes    ations    Minutes   Minute
19  --------- --------  --------  --------   --------  --------  --------
20  Minor       NA        NA        NA        NA        NA        NA
         A         B         C         D         E         F         G         H
21  Maj. Abd.   NA        NA        NA        NA        NA        NA
22  Maj. Oth.   NA        NA        NA        NA        NA        NA
23
24  Logic Section
25
26  Revenue - Room Charges
27  ----------------------
28
29  Type of              Total     Avg.      Total               Semi-
30  Patient              Expected  Stay      Days      Private   Private   Ward
31  ---------            --------------------------------------------------------
32  Surgical             NA        NA        NA        NA        NA        NA
33  --Room Rates                                       NA        NA        NA
34                                                     ------------------------------
35  --Revenues                                         NA        NA        NA
36                                                     ------------------------------
37                                                     ------------------------------
38  Medical              NA        NA        NA        NA        NA        NA
39  --Room Rates                                       NA        NA        NA
40                                                     ------------------------------
         A         B         C         D         E         F         G         H
41  --Revenues                                         NA        NA        NA
42                                                     ------------------------------
43                                                     ------------------------------
44  ----TOTALS                                         NA        NA        NA
45                                                     ------------------------------
46                                                     ------------------------------
47
```

	A	B	C	D	E	F	G	H
48	Revenue-Operating-Room Charges							
49	------------------------------							
50								
51	Type	Avg. #	Avg. #	Avg. #	#	Total	Rate Per	
52	Of	Of	Of	Of Man	Of Oper-	Man-	Man-	TOTAL
53	Operation	Minutes	People	Minutes	ations	Minutes	Minute	REVENUE
54	--------	--------	--------	--------	--------	--------	--------	--------
55	Minor	NA	NA	NA	NA	NA	NA	NA
56	Maj. Abd.	NA	NA	NA	NA	NA	NA	NA
57	Maj. Oth.	NA	NA	NA	NA	NA	NA	NA
58								--------
59								NA
60								--------

PROBLEM 10 - FLEXIBLE AND STATIC BUDGET

Wilkinson Company prepares budgets for each month of its fiscal
year. Budgeted amounts, along with actual results, are shown in
reports that are circulated to the managers whose operations are
being reported on and to their superiors. Excerpts from the
report of the latest two months for one production department are
given below:

	APRIL			MAY		
	BUDGET	ACTUAL	VARIANCE	BUDGET	ACTUAL	VARIANCE
Prod. in units	8,000	7,000	1,000	10,000	10,500	(500)
Costs:						
Material	$ 16,000	$14,600	$1,400	$ 20,000	$ 20,800	($800)
Dir. Labor	24,000	21,600	2,400	30,000	31,300	(1,300)
Ind. Labor	4,000	3,900	100	5,000	5,300	(300)
Power	7,000	6,700	300	8,000	8,400	(400)
Maint.	5,200	4,700	500	6,000	6,200	(200)
Supp. & Other	4,600	4,580	20	5,000	5,050	(50)
Total Costs	$60,800	$56,080	$4,720	$74,000	$77,050	($3,050)

Required:

1. Using the budgeted amounts, determine the fixed and variable
   components of each cost.

2. Prepare new reports showing in the budget columns the amounts
   of cost that you would expect to be incurred given the actual
   production achieved for April and May. Use the same format
   as is shown above.

3. Comment on the desirability of Wilkinson's methods of
   providing information to its managers. Please use a separate
   sheet of paper.

```
          A         B         C         D         E         F         G         H
1  PROBLEM TEN   FLEXIBLE AND STATIC BUDGET
2  TYPE:  C
3
4  NAME:        _____
5  DATE:        _____
6
7  Data Section
8
9  Requirement 1
10                                              Calculations
11
12                          BUDGET            CHANGE/    TOTAL
13                     High      Low           2000 =    COST    VARIABLE
14                    ----------------------  Var. Cost  AT      COST AT    FIXED
15  Units             10000     8000          Per unit   8000    8000     = AMOUNT
16                    (a)       (b)           (c)        (d)     (e)
17                                            (a-b)/2000  (b)    (cx8000)   (d-e)
18                    --------  --------      --------   ------  --------   --------
19  Mat.                                          2       16      16          0
20  D.L.                                          3       24      24          0
21  I.L.                                          .5      4       4           0
22  Power                                         .4      7.2     3.2         3
23  Maint.                                        .2      4.6     16          2
24  Supp.,Oth.                                                                3
25
26                    April     May
27  Actual prod.       NA        NA
28
29
30  Logic Section
31
32  Requirement 2              APRIL                         MAY
33                    -----------------------------  -----------------------------
34                    BUDGET    ACTUAL    VAR.       BUDGET    ACTUAL    VARIANCE
35                    --------  --------  --------   --------  --------  --------
36  Production
37    In Units
38
39
40  Costs:                                            T C      Vc at 7000    F
         A         B        C         D         E         F         G         H
41    Material                                 ___              ___         ___
42    Direct Labor                    1.77     14,6     12-4      22
43    Indirect Labor                  2.77              19.4      22
44    Power                           0.4      21,6               11
45    Maintenance                              3,9      2.8       33
46    Supplies &                      0.4857   6,7      3.4
47      Other                         0.4 285  1,7      3         17
48                                                      .94       36.4
49                                             4,58
50  TOTAL COSTS                       6.13424
```

45

PROBLEM 11   RETURN RATIOS AND LEVERAGE

The following selected data are taken from the financial statements of the Baxter Company:

Sales revenue	$ 650,000
Cost of goods sold	(400,000)
Gross profit	250,000
Selling, gen. & admin.	(100,000)
Operating income	150,000
Interest expense	50,000
Net income before taxes	100,000
Income tax expense (40%)	40,000
Net income	60,000
Accounts payable	$ 45,000
Accrued liabilities	70,000
Income taxes payable	10,000
Interest payable	25,000
Short-term loans pay.	150,000
Total current liabilities	300,000
Long-term bonds payable	500,000
Preferred stock, 10%, $100 par	250,000
Common stock, no par	600,000
Retained earnings	350,000
Total stockholders' equity	1,200,000
Total Liab. & S.E.	2,000,000

Required:

1. Compute the following ratios for the Baxter Company:
   a. Return on sales
   b. Asset turnover (assume total assets at the beginning of the year were $1,600,000)
   c. Return on assets
   d. Return on common stockholders' equity (assume that the only changes in stockholders' equity during the year were from the net income for the year and dividends on the preferred stock)
2. Comment on Baxter's use of leverage. Has the company successfully employed leverage? Explain your answer on a separate sheet of paper.

```
        A         B         C         D         E         F         G         H
1   PROBLEM ELEVEN   RETURN RATIOS AND LEVERAGE
2   Type: C
3
4   NAME:        _____
5   DATE:        _____
6
7   Data Section
8
9              Sales revenue        NA
10             COGS                 NA
11             Sell,Gen.&Admin.     NA
12             Int. Exp.            NA
13             Inc. Tax Exp.        NA
14             Accts. Pay.          NA
15             Accrued Liab.        NA
16             Inc. tax. pay.       NA
17             Int. Pay.            NA
18             S.T. loans pay.      NA
19             L.T. bonds pay.      NA
20             Pref. Stock          NA
21         Common Stock             NA
22         Retained Earnings        NA
23
24
25
26  Logic Section
27
28  1a. Return on sales             NA
29  1b. Asset turnover              NA
30  1c. Return on assets            NA
31  1d. Return on C.S.Equity        NA
32
33
34
35
36
37
38
39
40
```

PROBLEM 12   PRODUCTION AND CASH DISBURSEMENTS BUDGETS

The following data relate to the Corr Company and its single product, a desk lamp:

(a) Sales forecast, January through June, 19x9 (in units): 1,200; 1,400; 1,700; 2,000; 2,400; and 1,800.
(b) Inventory policy: inventory is maintained at 150% of budgeted sales needs for the coming month.
(c) Cost data: materials $7 per unit; direct labor $7 per unit; and variable overhead $5 per unit.
(d) Materials are purchased daily and are paid for in the following month; all other costs requiring cash disbursements are paid as incurred.
(e) The beginning inventory for January is 1,500 units.

Required:
A. 1. Prepare a budget of production for each month of the period for which you have data. (in units).
    2. Prepare a budget of cash disbursements for each month for which you have data. Production in December 19x8 was 1,200 units.
B. Prepare the above budgets assuming that the inventory policy is 120% of budgeted sales needs for the coming month.
C. What are the implications of this change of inventory policy?

PROBLEM 13   CASH RECEIPTS AND CASH BUDGET -Continuation of PROBLEM 12.

Refer to the original data in Problem 12.   The lamp sells for $25 per unit.   All sales are on account with 40% collected in the month of sale, 60% in the month after sale. Sales in December 19X8 were 1,000 units.

Required:

1. Prepare a schedule of budgeted cash receipts for each of the months for which you have data.
2. Prepare a cash budget for each month for which you have data. Cash at January 1 is $8,000.

```
              A         B          C        D      E      F      G      H        I
 1    PROBLEM TWELVE   PRODUCTION AND CASH DISBURSEMENTS BUDGETS
 2    TYPE:   B
 3
 4    NAME:        _____
 5    DATE:        _____
 6
 7    Data Section
 8
 9    Production Budget, In Units for Sales:
10
11                              Jan    Feb    Mar    Apr    May
12    Sales forecast            NA     NA     NA     NA     NA
13
14    Inv. % of sales*          NA
15    Mat. cost/unit            NA
16    Direct labor              NA
17    Var. O.H.                 NA
18    Beg. Inv. - Jan.          NA
19    Production - December     NA
20    Selling price/unit        NA
21    Collection percentages:
22      Month of sale           NA
23      Month after sale        NA
24    December sales            NA
25    Cash balance -Jan.1       NA
26
27
28    *Please enter a decimal.
29
30    Logic section
31
32                              Jan    Feb    Mar    Apr    May    TOTALS
33                              ------------------------------------------
34    Ending Inventory          NA     NA     NA     NA     NA     NA
35    Sales                     NA     NA     NA     NA     NA     NA
36                              ------------------------------------------
37    Requirements              NA     NA     NA     NA     NA     NA
38    Beginning Inventory       NA     NA     NA     NA     NA     NA
39                              ------------------------------------------
40    Production                NA     NA     NA     NA     NA     NA
              A         B          C        D      E      F      G      H        I
41                              ------------------------------------------
42                              ------------------------------------------
43    Cash Disbursements - Budget
44    --------------------------
45                              Jan    Feb    Mar    Apr    May    TOTALS
46                              ------------------------------------------
47    Materials-($7*Prior Month
48         Production)          NA     NA     NA     NA     NA     NA
49    Other Variable-($12*Current
50         Month Production)    NA     NA     NA     NA     NA     NA
51                              ------------------------------------------
52    TOTALS                    NA     NA     NA     NA     NA     NA
53
```

```
54
55
56   PROBLEM THIRTEEN   CASH RECEIPTS BUDGET AND CASH BUDGET
57   Cash Receipts Budget
58   --------------------           Jan   Feb   Mar   Apr   May   TOTALS
59                                 -----------------------------------------
60   Sales (@ $25/Unit)             NA    NA    NA    NA    NA    NA

          A         B         C     D     E     F     G     H     I
61                                 -----------------------------------------
62   Receipts:
63     Current Month (40%)          NA    NA    NA    NA    NA    NA
64     Prior Month (60%)            NA    NA    NA    NA    NA    NA
65                                 -----------------------------------------
66   TOTAL RECEIPTS                 NA    NA    NA    NA    NA    NA
67                                 -----------------------------------------
68                                 -----------------------------------------
69
70
71   Cash Budget
72   -----------                    Jan   Feb   Mar   Apr   May  TOTALS
73
74   Beginning Balance              NA    NA    NA    NA    NA    NA
75   Receipts                       NA    NA    NA    NA    NA    NA
76                                 -----------------------------------------
77   Available                      NA    NA    NA    NA    NA    NA
78   Disbursements                  NA    NA    NA    NA    NA    NA
79                                 -----------------------------------------
80   Ending Balance                 NA    NA    NA    NA    NA    NA
81                                 -----------------------------------------
82                                 -----------------------------------------
```

PROBLEM 14   COMPREHENSIVE BUDGET

Following is the balance sheet of your firm. Arlon Industries, at December 31, 19X5. Also shown is a projected income statement for the first three months of 19X6, prepared by your chief accountant. You are happy with the projection and gloat about it to your banker. The Banker, always eager to lend money, has asked if you will need any cash to get through the first quarter. "Of course not" is your reply. Later, back at your office, the chief accountant informs you of the following:

1. Sales are all on credit and are collected 50% in the month of sale, 50% in the month after sale.
2. It is company policy to build up inventory so that inventory is always equal to the next two months' sales in units. However, at December 31, 19X5 your inventory is depleted because of the dock strike.
3. You pay for purchases 50% in the month of purchase, 50% in the following month.
4. You are committed to paying the recorded cash dividend of $2,000 in March.
5. All cash expenses are paid in the month incurred, except for purchases.
6. The accounts receivable at December 31, 19X5 will be collected in January; the Accounts payable at December 31, 19X5 will be paid in January.
7. The monthly breakdown of projected sales is as follows: January, $20,000; February, $30,000; and March, $50,000. In addition, April sales are expected to be $20,000, and May sales $20,000.
8. Cash should not go below $5,000.

ARCON INDUSTRIES
BALANCE SHEET
December 31, 19X5

Cash	$ 5,000		Accounts payable	$16,000	
Acct.Rec.	10,000		Div. payable	2,000	$18,000
Inventory	24,000	$ 39,000	Owner's equity		61,000
Plant&Equip					
net		40,000			
Total Assets		$ 79,000	Total Liab.& O.E.		$ 79,000

BUDGETED INCOME STATEMENT
Three Months Ending March 31, 19X6

Sales(10,000units @ $10)		$100,000
Cost of sales (10,000 units @ $6)		60,000
Gross profit		40,000
Operating expenses:		
Wages & Salaries	$9,000	
Rent	3,000	
Depreciation	3,000	
Other expenses	1,500	16,500
Income		$ 23,500

Required: Do you regret your reply to your banker? Explain by preparing the appropriate schedules. (If borrowings are necessary, assume that they are in $1,000 multiples at the beginning of the month and that repayments are at the end of months with 12% annual interest on the amount repaid.)

What impact would changing the company's inventory policy to one-half of the next two months sales have on your reply?

```
          A         B          C          D           E           F           G           H
1   PROBLEM FOURTEEN   COMPREHENSIVE BUDGET
2   Name:  NA
3   Date:  NA
4   Type:  C
5
6   Data Section
7
8   Collections on sales:
9     % in month of sale*               NA
10    % in month after sale*            NA
11  Inventory, Dec. 31, 19X5            NA
12  Cash, Dec. 31, 19X5                 NA
13  Accts. Rec., Dec. 31, 19X5          NA
14  Accts. Pay., Dec. 31, 19X5          NA
15  Div. payable, Dec. 31, 19X5         NA
16  Budgeted exp., Three months
17      ending March 31, 19X5:     Jan.        Feb.        March
18        Wages & Salaries          NA          NA          NA
19        Rent                      NA          NA          NA
20        Deprec.                   NA          NA          NA
          A         B          C          D           E           F           G           H
21        Other                     NA          NA          NA
22  Cost of Sales %*                 NA          NA          NA
23  Payment on purchases:
24    % in month of purchase*        NA
25    % in month after purchase      NA
26  Minimum Cash balance             NA
27  Borrowings in multiples of       NA
28  Borrowing rate of interest       NA
29  *Please insert decimal.
30
31
32                             Jan.        Feb.        March       April       May
33  Projected sales:            NA          NA          NA          NA          NA
34
35
36  CASH RECEIPTS BUDGET
37  -------------------
38                             Jan.        Feb.        March       TOTAL
39                             -------     -------     -------     -------
40  Prior Month's Sales         NA          NA          NA          NA
41  Current Month's Sales       NA          NA          NA          NA
42                             -------     -------     -------     -------
43    Total receipts            NA          NA          NA          NA
44
```

	A	B	C	D	E	F	G	H
45	PURCHASES BUDGET			Jan.	Feb.	March	TOTAL	
46	---------------			NA	NA	NA	NA	
47	Desired Ending Inventory			NA	NA	NA	NA	
48	Cost of Sales			NA	NA	NA	NA	
49				-------	-------	-------	-------	
50	Total Requirements			NA	NA	NA	NA	
51	Beginning Inventory			NA	NA	NA	NA	
52				-------	-------	-------	-------	
53	Purchases			NA	NA	NA	NA	
54								
55	CASH DISBURSEMENTS BUDGET							
56	-------------------------			Jan.	Feb.	March	TOTAL	
57	Purchases:			NA	NA	NA	NA	
58	--Current Month			NA	NA	NA	NA	
59	--Prior Month							
60				-------------------------------------				
	A	B	C	D	E	F	G	H
61	Other Costs:			NA	NA	NA	NA	
62	--Wages and Salaries			NA	NA	NA	NA	
63	--Rent			NA	NA	NA	NA	
64	--Other			NA	NA	NA	NA	
65	Dividends							
66				-------------------------------------				
67	Totals			NA	NA	NA	NA	
68								
69	CASH BUDGET							
70	-----------			Jan.	Feb.	March	TOTAL	
71	Beginning Balance			NA	NA	NA	NA	
72	Receipts			NA	NA	NA	NA	
73				-------------------------------------				
74	Total Available			NA	NA	NA	NA	
75	Disbursements			NA	NA	NA	NA	
76				-------------------------------------				
77	Indicated Balance			NA	NA	NA	NA	
78								
79	Minimum Balance			NA	NA	NA	NA	
80	Excess (Deficiency)			NA	NA	NA	NA	
	A	B	C	D	E	F	G	H
81	Borrowings			NA	NA	NA	NA	
82	Repayments			NA	NA	NA	NA	
83	Months debt outstanding			NA	NA	NA		
84	Interest			NA	NA	NA	NA	
85	Ending Balance			NA	NA	NA	NA	
86								
87								
88								
89								
90								

PROBLEM 15 - BUDGETING EQUATIONS (CMA adapted)

Your firm has just acquired a new computer, and one of the first things that the president wants it to be used for is the preparations of the firm's comprehensive budget. He assigns you the task of formulating a set of equations that can be used to write a program to perform the computations required for the budgets. You consult with the chief programmer, and the two of you decide that the following notation should be used, which will make it easy for the programmer to prepare the necessary programs.

$S-o$ = sales in current month (units)
$S+1$ = sales in coming month (units)
$S-1$ = sales in prior month (units)
$S-2$ = sales in second prior month (units)
P   = selling price per unit
CGS   = cost of goods sold per unit (purchase price0
OVC   = other variable costs per unit
FC   = total fixed costs per month
FCC   = fixed costs per month requiring cash disbursements
PUR   = purchases in current month (units)
PUR-1= purchases in prior month (units)

You examine the records of the firm and decide that the firm's policies or experienced relationships are as follows:

1. Collections on sales are 30% in the month of sale, 50% in the month after sale, and 20% in the second month after sale.
2. Inventory is maintained at twice the coming month's budgeted sales volume.
3. Purchases are paid for 60% in the month after purchase and 40% in the month of purchase.
4. All other costs are paid as incurred.

Required:

A. Prepare equations that can be used to budget for the following:
    1. Income for the current month.
    2. Cash receipts in current month.
    3. Purchases in current month in units.
    4. Purchases in current month in dollars.
    5. Cash disbursements in current month.

B. What are the advantages of this type of computer analysis over hand-calculating budgets? (Please answer on separate sheet of paper.)

```
        A         B         C         D         E         F         G         H
1   PROBLEM FIFTEEN   BUDGETING EQUATIONS
2   NAME:        _____
3   DATE:        _____
4   TYPE:   C
5
6   Data Section
7
8                   (SO) =SALES IN CURRENT MONTH (UNITS)
9                   (S1) =SALES IN COMING MONTH (UNITS)
10                 (S-1) =SALES IN PRIOR MONTH (UNITS)
11                 (S-2) =SALES IN SECOND PRIOR MONTH (UNITS)
12                   (P) =SELLING PRICE PER UNIT
13                 (CGS) =COST OF GOODS SOLD PER UNIT
14                  (FC) =TOTAL FIXED COSTS PER MONTH
15                 (FCC) =FIXED COSTS PER MONTH REQUIRING CASH DISBURSEMENTS
16                 (PUR) =PURCHASES IN CURRENT MONTH (UNITS)
17               (PUR-1) =PURCHASES IN PRIOR MONTH (UNITS)
18   Collections on sales:
19     In month of sale*              NA .3
20     In month after sale*          NA .5  51
        A         B         C         D         E         F         G         H
21     In 2nd month after sale*      NA ,2
22     Inventory -as % of sales      NA 200% x
23   Payment of purchases:
24     In month of purchase*         NA .4
25     In month after purchase*      NA .6
26   *Please enter a decimal.
27
28   Logic Section
29
30   REQUIRED:(Enter a single quote "'" before the formulas so Lotus will
31            recognize that the formulas are labels and will print them.
32            Otherwise Lotus would attempt to solve them and report "@na"
33            since the values are not available.)
34       1.          NA  SOxCOGS -FC = Iven
35       2.          NA  .3 current .5 after - Slea
36       3.          NA  COSS + IL - BI purch
37       4.          NA
38       5.          NA  .4 current + .6 prior check for current
39
40
```

1. SO x P -(SO)(CGS) -SO ovc -FC

2. -.360xP + -5(S-1)xP + .2(S-2)xP

3. CGS + 2(S+1) - 2(SO)

4. CGS*SO + 2(S+1)xP - 2(SO)P

5. FCC + 0.4(Pur(CGS)) + 0.6(Pur-1)CGS

56

PROBLEM 16 BASIC WORKING CAPITAL INVESTMENT

The managers of DeCosmo Enterprises are considering a new product. They expect to be able to sell 50,000 units annually for the next five years at $7 each. Variable costs are expected to be $3 per unit, annual fixed costs requiring cash disbursements $80,000. The product requires machinery and equipment costing $150,000 with a 5-year life and no salvage value. The firm would use straight-line depreciation. Additionally, accounts receivable would increase about $60,000, inventory about $20,000. These amounts would be returned in full at the end of the five years. The tax rate is 40% and cost of capital is 16%.

Required:

1.   Determine the net present value of the investment.

2.   Cost of capital is 14%. Does this alter your decision? (Please answer on a separate sheet of paper.)

Notes to students. This template allows you to solve the problem using 1) the present value factors found in your text and/or 2) Lotus' NPV function. If you wish to only use the tables solve only the first 2 columns of the spreadsheet. If you wish to use the NPV function of Lotus solve the third column as well. (I'd suggest you do both methods and check the answers to each other.)
     The format of the @NPV function is as follows @NPV(x,range). The X refers to the rate of return and the range refers to the cash flows over a certain number of years excluding the initial investment. In our problem the range of cash flows in years 1 through 5 can be found in the range G39 to G43. (Note, this cash flow should also reflect the return of working capital in year 5.) Follow the format above and see if you can find the present value in cell G44.

```
          A         B         C         D         E         F         G         H
1   PROBLEM SIXTEEN   BASIC WORKING CAPITAL INVESTMENT
2   TYPE: C
3
4   NAME:        _____
5   DATE:        _____
6
7   Data Section
8                                           Year 1    Year 2    Year 3    Year 4    Year 5
9   Projected units sold              NA        NA        NA        NA        NA
10  S.P. per unit            NA
11  V.C. per unit            NA
12  Annual Fixed Costs       NA
13  Initial Investments:
14    Mach. & Equip          NA
15    Accounts Rec.          NA
16    Inventory              NA
17  Salvage value            NA
18  Investment Life          NA (years)
19  Tax Rate*                NA
20  Cost of Capital*         NA
          A         B         C         D         E         F         G         H
21
22    *Please enter decimals.
23                                                CASH-FLOWS          CASH-FLOWS
24                                                Using               Using
25                                      TAX    NPV Tables          Lotus' @NPV
26                                   --------  ---------          -----------
27
28  Contribution Margin               NA        NA
29  Cash Fixed Costs                  NA        NA
30                                   --------  ---------
31  Pretax CAsh Flow                  NA        NA
32  Depreciation                      NA
33                                   --------
34  Increased Pretax Income           NA
35  Income Tax-@40%                   NA        NA      (Lotus needs a range of
36                                           --------      cash flows to refer to.
37  Net Cash Flow                               NA
38  Present Value Factor                        NA    Year    Cash Flows
39                                           ---------   1           NA
40  Present Value of Flows                      NA       2           NA
          A         B         C         D         E         F         G         H
41  Present Value of Return of                          3           NA
42    Working Capital                           NA      4           NA
43                                           --------    5           NA
44  Total Present Value                          NA P.Value         NA
45  Investment                                   NA Invest.         NA
46                                           ---------
47  Net Present Value                            NA N.P.V.          NA
48                                           ---------
49                                           ---------
50
```

PROBLEM 17   EFFECTS OF ALLOCATIONS

Grange Company has two service departments: building services
and administration.   The firm has three operating departments.
Some data associated with the operating departments are presented
below.

Operating Departments

	A	B	C
Square feet of space occupied	5,000	7,500	12,500
Machine-hours worked	42,000	70,000	88,000
Sales value of production	$1,200,000	$1,000,000	$1,800,000

Costs for the service departments are as follows: building
services $160,000; administrative $300,000.

Required:

1.   Allocate service department costs on three different bases.

2.   Comment on the results in part 1 above.

```
         A          B          C          D          E          F          G          H
 1  PROBLEM SEVENTEEN   EFFECTS OF ALLOCATIONS
 2  Name:  NA
 3  Date:  NA
 4  Type:  B
 5
 6  Data Section
 7                                        A          B          C
 8  Square feet occupied                 NA         NA         NA
 9  Machine-hours worked                 NA         NA         NA
10  Sales value of production            NA         NA         NA
11
12                                 Building
13                                 Services    Admin.
14  Service Dept. Costs               NA         NA
15
16  Logic Section
17
18  1.   ALLOCATION BASED ON SQUARE FOOTAGE:
19
20                                 Building
         A          B          C          D          E          F          G          H
21  Operating Department           Services   Admin.      TOTAL
22  --------------------           --------  -------     -------
23
24  Department A                      NA         NA         NA
25  Department B                      NA         NA         NA
26  Department C                      NA         NA         NA
27                                 --------  --------   --------
28    TOTALS                          NA         NA         NA
29
30
31  2.   ALLOCATION BASED ON MACHINE HOURS:
32
33                                 Building
34  Operating Department           Services   Admin.      TOTAL
35  --------------------           --------  -------     -------
36
37  Department A                      NA         NA         NA
38  Department B                      NA         NA         NA
39  Department C                      NA         NA         NA
40       A          B          C      --------  --------   --------
         D          E          F          G          H
41    TOTALS                          NA         NA         NA
42
43
44  3.   ALLOCATION BASED ON SALES VALUES:
45
46                                 Building
47  Operating Department           Services   Admin.      TOTAL
48  --------------------           --------  -------     -------
49
50  Department A                      NA         NA         NA
51  Department B                      NA         NA         NA
52  Department C                      NA         NA         NA
53                                 --------  --------   --------
54    TOTALS                          NA         NA         NA
55
56
```

60

PROBLEM 18 PERFORMANCE REPORTING-ALTERNATIVE ORGANIZATIONAL STRUCTURE (CMA adapted)

Cranwell Company sells three products in a foreign market and a domestic market. An income statement for the first month of 19X2 shows the following results:

Sales		$1,300,000
Cost of goods sold		1,110,000
Gross profit		290,000
Selling expenses	$105,000	
Administrative expenses	72,000	177,000
Income		$ 113,000

Data regarding the two markets and three products are given below.

	Products		
	A	B	C
Sales:			
Domestic	$400,000	$300,000	$300,000
Foreign	100,000	100,000	100,000
Total sales	500,000	400,000	400,000
Var. prod. costs (% of sales)	60%	70%	60%
Var. sell. costs (% of sales)	3%	2%	2%

Product A is made in a single factory that incurs fixed costs (included in cost of goods sold) of $48,000 per month. Products B and C are made in a single factory and require the same machinery. Monthly fixed production costs at that factory are $142,000.

Fixed selling expenses are joint to the three products, but $36,000 is separable with respect to the domestic market and $38,000 to the foreign market. All administrative expenses are fixed. About $25,000 is traceable to the foreign market, $35,000 to the domestic market.

Required:
1. Assume that Cranwell has separate managers responsible for each market. Prepare performance reports for the domestic and foreign markets.

2. Assume that Cranwell has separate managers responsible for each product. Prepare performance reports for the three products.

3. What is the advantage of each analysis? (Please answer on a separate sheet of paper.)

```
        A          B          C          D          E          F          G          H
1   PROBLEM EIGHTEEN   PERFORMANCE REPORTING-ALTERNATIVE ORGANIZATIONAL STRUC
2   Type:  C
3
4   NAME:        _____
5   DATE:        _____
6
7   Data Section
8                              A          B          C      Total
9   Sales:
10     Domestic             NA         NA         NA
11     Foreign              NA         NA         NA
12  Var. prod. costs*       NA         NA         NA
13  Var. sell. costs*       NA         NA         NA
14  Fixed expenses:
15     Selling-joint                                       NA
16     Selling - Domestic                                  NA
17     Selling - Foreign                                   NA
18     Administrative - joint                              NA
19     Administrative - Foreign                            NA
20     Administrative - Domestic                           NA
        A          B          C          D          E          F          G          H
21     COGS - traceable to A                               NA
22     COGS - B & C                                        NA
23     Monthly production                                  NA
24  * As a percentage of sales.
25
26  1.                                              INCOME STATEMENT
27                                                  BY MARKET
28                                                  March  19X2
29
30                                                  Domestic  Foreign  TOTAL
31                                                  --------  --------  --------
32
33  Sales
34  Variable Cost of Sales
35  Variable Selling Costs
36
37  Total Variable Costs
38
39  Contribution Margin
40  Traceable Fixed Costs:
        A          B          C          D          E          F          G          H
41  --Selling
42  --Administrative
43
44  Total Traceable
45
46  Margin Earned by Market
47
48  Joint Costs
49
50  Income
```

```
51
52                                  INCOME STATEMENT
53                                     BY MARKET
54                                    March  19X2
55
56                                             PRODUCT
57                               --------  --------  --------
58                                  A         B         C        TOTAL
59                               --------  --------  --------  --------
60
            A          B          C          D         E         F         G          H
61   Sales
62   Variable Costs:
63   --Cost of Sales
64   --Selling
65
66   Total Variable Costs
67
68   Contribution Margin
69
70   Traceable Fixed Costs:
71   --Production
72
73   Product Margin
74
75   Joint Costs:
76   --Selling
77   --Administrative
78   --Production
79
80   Total Joint Costs
81
82    Income
83
84
```

PROBLEM 19   TRANSFER PRICES AND GOAL CONGRUENCE (CMA adapted)
A.R. Oma Company manufactures a line of men's perfumes and aftershave lotions.   The manufacturing process is a series of mixing operations with the adding of aromatic and coloring ingredients. The finished product is bottled and packed in cases of six bottles each.

The bottles are made by one division, which was bought several years ago.   The management believed that the appeal of the product was partly due to the attractiveness of the bottles and so has spent a great deal of time and effort developing new types of bottles and new processes for making them.

The bottle division has been selling all of its output to the manufacturing division at market-based transfer prices.   The price has been determined by asking other bottle manufacturers for bids on the bottles of the appropriate size and in the required quantities.   At present, the firm has received the following bids from outsiders, for a year's supply.

Quantity Case of 6 Bottles	Price Price per Case	Total Price
2,000,000	$2.00	$ 4,000,000
4,000,000	1.75	7,600,000
6,000,000	1.6666	10,000,000

The bottle division has fixed costs of $1,200,000 per year and variable costs of $1 per case.   Both divisions are treated as investment centers and their managers receive significant bonuses based on profitability, so the transfer price to be used is of great interest to both of them.

The perfume manufacturing division has variable costs, excluding the cost of bottles, of $8 per case and fixed costs of $4,000,000 annually.   The market research group has determined that the following price-volume relationships are likely to prevail during the coming year.

Sales Volume in cases	Selling Price per case	Total Revenue
2,000,000	$12.50	$25,000,000
4,000,000	11.40	45,600,000
6,000,000	10.65	63,900,000

The president of the firm believes that the market-based transfer price should be used in pricing transfers.   The bottle division has no outside sales potential because the firm does not wish to supple competitors with its own highly appealing bottles.

Required:

1.   Of the three levels of volume given, determine the one that will provide the highest profit to the (a) bottle division, (b) perfume division, (c) firm as a whole.

2. Do the results in part 1 contradict your understanding of the effectiveness of market-based transfer prices: Explain why or why not.
3. Make a recommendation to the president of the firm.

```
        A         B         C         D         E         F         G         H
 1  NINE-TEEN  TRANSFER PRICES AND GOAL CONGRUENCE
 2  Type:  C
 3
 4  NAME:         _____
 5  DATE:         _____
 6
 7  Data Section
 8
 9  Quantity                              2000000   4000000   6000000
10    Price/case                               NA        NA        NA
11    Sell. Price/case                         NA        NA        NA
12  Bottle Division:
13    Fixed costs                    NA
14    Var. costs/case                NA
15  Perfume Division:
16    Fixed costs                    NA
17    Var. costs/case                NA
18
19  Logic Section
20
        A         B         C         D         E         F         G         H
21  1 A.)
22                                                        VOLUMES
23                                        --------  --------  --------
24                                        2000000   4000000   6000000
25                                        --------  --------  --------
26  Revenue
27  Variable Costs
28                                        --------  --------  --------
29  Contribution Margin
30  Fixed Costs
31                                        --------  --------  --------
32  Divisional Profit
33                                        ========  ========  ========
34    B.)                                                VOLUMES
35                                        --------  --------
36                                        2000000   4000000   6000000
37                                        --------  --------  --------
38
39  Revenue
40  Variable Costs:
        A         B         C         D         E         F         G         H
41    Bottles
42    Other
43                                        --------  --------  --------
44  Total Variable Costs
45                                        --------  --------  --------
46  Contribution Margin
47  Fixed Costs
48                                        --------  --------  --------
49  Divisional Profit
50                                        ========  ========  ========
51
```

```
52    C.)                                          VOLUMES
53                               --------  --------  --------
54                               2000000   4000000   6000000
55                               --------  --------  --------
56    Profit:
57      Bottle Division
58      Perfume Division
59                               --------  --------  --------
60    Total Profit
         A        B        C        D        E        F        G        H
61                               ========  ========  ========
62                                            OR
63
64                                          VOLUMES
65                               --------  --------  --------
66                               2000000   4000000   6000000
67                               --------  --------  --------
68    Sales:  Perfume Only
69    Variable Costs:
70      Perfume
71      Bottles
72                               --------  --------  --------
73    Total Variable Costs
74                               --------  --------  --------
75    Contribution Margin
76    Fixed Costs
77                               --------  --------  --------
78    Profits
79                               ========  ========  ========
80
```

PROBLEM 20 - VARIANCE ANALYSIS

Kuhn Company makes automobile antifreeze. The firm has developed the following formula for budgeting monthly factory overhead costs. Total overhead cost =$140,000 + ($10 x direct labor hours). Other data relating to the cost of a case of the product are given below.

Materials	6 gallons at $1.50 per gallon
Direct labor	1/2 hour at $8 per hour

During a recent month Kuhn produced 12,000 cases of product and incurred the following costs.

Materials (purchases and used)	59,500 gallons	$ 48,200
Direct labor	5,100 hours	$ 30,600
Overhead		$ 183,500

Required:

1.   Compute the price and quantity variance for materials and direct labor and the total variance for overhead.

2.   Compute the above requirements assuming the following costs.
Materials (purchased and used)	73,500 gallons	$106,575
Direct labor	5,800 hours	$ 48,300
Overhead		$183,500

3.   What can you conclude about the two variances completed in 1. and 2. above.   (Try to relate variances whenever possible.) Please answer on a separate sheet of paper.

```
         A           B           C          D          E          F          G
1   PROBLEM TWENTY   VARIANCE ANALYSIS
2   Type  B
3
4   NAME:           _____
5   DATE:           _____
6
7   Data Section
8
9   Actual  Price/Gallon                          NA  0.8100 84
10  Actual  Gallons Used/Case                     NA  4.958
11  Standard Price/Gallon                         NA  1.50
12  Standard Gallons Allowed                      NA  72000
13  Actual  Hours Worked                          NA  5100
14  Actual  Rate/Hour                             NA  6.00
15  Standard Hours Allowed/Case                   NA  .5
16  Standard Rate/Hour                            NA  8
17  Cases Produced                                NA  12000
18  Actual  Overhead                              NA  183500
19  Standard Fixed Overhead                       NA
20  Standard Rate - Overhead                      NA
         A           B           C          D          E          F          G
21
22
23  Logic Section
24
25  MATERIALS VARIANCE:
26  -------------------
27
28  Std Price  Act Price  Total Price          Std.Price  Std. Price   Total
29     *          *          Rate                 *          *       Quantity
30  Act Hrs.   Act Hrs.    Variance           Std Hrs.   Act Hrs.    Variance
31  ---------------------------------          -----------------------------
32  84250 NA   48200 NA    4050  NA            108000 NA   84250 NA    18750 NA
33
34
35  LABOR VARIANCE
36  --------------
37   Std Rate   Act Rate    Total              Std Rate   Std Rate    Total
38     *          *          Rate                 *          *       Quantity
39  Act Hrs.   Act Hrs     Variance           Std Hrs.   Act Hrs.    Variance
40  ---------------------------------   D      -----------------------------
    4080 A     3060 B      10200 C             4800 E     4080 F      720 G
41
42      NA         NA          NA                 NA         NA          NA
43
44
45  OVERHEAD VARIANCE
46  -----------------
47
48   Std Rate    Total       Total
49     *         Actual     Overhead
50  Act Hrs.   Overhead     Variance
51  ---------------------------------
52      NA         NA          NA
53    191000     183500      7500
54
```

PROBLEM 21 - DETERMINING A BASE FOR COST STANDARDS

The production manager of Wingate Company recently performed a study to see how many units of product could be made by a worker who had no interruptions, always had materials available as needed, made no errors, and worked at peak speed for an entire hour. A worker could make 20 units in an hour under these ideal conditions. In the past, about 15 units per hour was the actual average output. However, some new materials handling equipment had recently been purchased and the manager is confident that an average of 17 units per hour could be achieved by nearly all of the workers.

All workers are paid $8.50 per hour. During the month after the study workers were paid $850,000 for 100,000 hours. Production was 1,650,000 units.

Required:

1. Compute the standard labor cost per unit to the nearest tenth of a cent based on the following:
   (a) historical performance
   (b) ideal performance
   (c) currently attainable performance

2. Compute the labor efficiency variance under each of the standards in part 1 above and comment on the results. Which method of setting the standard would you choose for planning purposes? For control purposes? Explain.

```
         A        B        C        D        E        F        G        H
1   PROBLEM TWENTY-ONE   DETERMINING A BASE FOR COSTS STANDARDS
2   Type:  C
3
4   NAME:        _____
5   DATE:        _____
6
7   Data Section
8                                                   Hist.    Ideal    C. Attain.
9   Standard Units/Hour                              NA       NA        NA
10  Wage/Hour                         NA
11  Hours Worked                      NA
12  Prod.-Units                       NA
13
14  Logic Section
15
16  1.)   COMPUTATION OF STANDARD COST FOR LABOR
17
18                                          Wage Rate  Units  Standard
19                                          Per Hour  Per Hour  Cost
20                                          --------  --------  --------
         A        B        C        D        E        F        G        H
21  Historical Performance
22  Ideal Performance
23  Currently Attainable Performance
24
25  2.)   COMPUTATION OF VARIANCES
26                                          Production *        Actual
27                                          Standard Cost        Cost   Variance
28                                          -------------       --------  --------
29  Historical Performance
30  Ideal Performance
31  Currently Attainable Performance
32
33
```

PROBLEM 22 - JOB COSTING IN A SERVICE FIRM

Russell and Morrison is a firm of architectural engineers operating in a single office in a medium-sized city. The firm charges clients for the time that each person on the staff spends on the client's business, using a rate of 2 1/2 times the person's salary, based on an 1,800-hour working year. Thus, an architectural draftsman earning a salary of $15,000 would be charged out to clients at $21 per hour (($15,000/1,800)x2.5=$20.83, rounded to $21). The rate is intended to cover all costs as well as yield a profit to the firm.

Budgeted results for 19X9 are as follows:

Salaries of profession staff	$ 700,000
Salaries of support personnel(clerks,etc.)	78,000
Other costs	680,000
Total expected costs	$ 1,458,000

The listed costs do not include any salaries for Russell and Morrison. Each partner expects to work about 1,200 chargeable hours and to bill those hours at a rate of $60 per hour. About 80% of the time of professional staff is chargeable to clients, about 40% of the time of support personnel. The nonchargeable time is for general firm business, professional activities (attending seminars and continuing-education programs), and the like.

Required:
1. What income should the partners earn, in total, if their estimates of costs and performed services prove correct:

2. Suppose that two specific professional employees work on the architectural design for a particular client. One earns $18,000 per year, the other $21,000, and each works 12 hours on this particular project. How much will the firm charge the client for the project assuming that neither the partners nor the support staff is involved in this project? (Round hourly rates to the nearest dollar.)

3. What do you conclude about the method Russell and Morrison uses to charge clients?

```
      A          B          C          D          E          F          G          H
1  PROBLEM TWENTY-TWO   JOB COSTING IN A SERVICE FIRM
2  Type:  B
3                    Seth + Doll
4  NAME:            May 3, 99
5  DATE:
6
7  Data Section
8                                        Prof.      Support      R.&M. 57,600
9  Budgeted Salaries                  70NA000  NA  78,000  NA    NA
10 Charg. Hours %                       .8 NA        .4 NA        NA  1.00
11 Billing Rate              NA                                   NA
12 Base Year Hours           NA
13 Estimated Hours)          NA
14 Other Exp.                NA
15 Chargeable Hours          NA
16
17 Part 2 - data                    1st person            2nd person
18 Salaries                              NA                    NA
19 Hours worked                          NA                    NA
20
      A          B          C          D          E          F          G          H
21 Logic Section
22
23 1.)
24
25 Revenue:
26 --Professional Staff                  NA
27 --Support Staff                       NA
28 --Russel and Morrison                 NA  576,000
29                                    --------
30 Total                                 NA
31 Salaries                              NA
32 Other Expenses                        NA
33                                    --------
34 Income                                NA
35                                    ========
36 2.)
37         Hourly Rates              r   NA
38                                   :   NA
39                                   ---------
40         Total                     12  NA
      A          B          C          D          E          F          G          H
41         Hours Worked               10NA
42                                   ---------
43         Charge                    2   NA   8205
44                                   ---------
45                                   ---------
46
```